A YOUNG PERSON'S GUIDE TO THE TWELVE STEPS

Stephen Roos

Hazelden
Center City, Minnesota 55012-0176

Library of Congress Cataloging-in-Publication Data
Roos, Stephen.
    A young person's guide to the twelve steps/Stephen Roos.
        p.   cm.
    Summary: Introduces twelve-step programs designed to
help people recover from substance abuse and other addic-
tive behavior, using alcoholism as an example.
    ISBN 978-0-89486-851-1
    1. Teenagers—Conduct of life. 2. Twelve-step programs.
3. Teenagers—Alcohol use. 4. Alcoholics—Rehabilitation.
[1. Twelve-step programs. 2. Alcoholism—Treatment.
3. Substance abuse—Treatment.] I. Title.
BJ1661.R64 1992
362.29'186'0835—dc20

                                                    92-21818
                                                        CIP
                                                         AC

A YOUNG PERSON'S GUIDE TO THE TWELVE STEPS

About the book

A take-it-along companion, *A Young Person's Guide to the Twelve Steps* is just the right size to put in your jeans' pocket and take to read on the bus, over the lunch hour, at the beach. Can the Twelve Steps work for young people? How do you use them to recover from addiction? Or to cope with stressful situations with friends, siblings, and dates? These and many other issues are presented here in terms you can not only learn from but also enjoy. Each of the Twelve Steps is covered through the eyes of young people, taking advantage of Stephen Roos's intimate knowledge of and passion for the good life of recovery.

About the author

Stephen Roos was born in New York City and grew up in Connecticut. He graduated from Yale and worked in publishing before becoming a professional writer. In addition to the Maple Street Kids stories, which are published by Hazelden, Roos is the author of the New Eden Kids series and the Pet Lovers Club books. He makes his home in New York State's Hudson River Valley.

CONTENTS

WELCOME

Ever since the Twelve Steps were formulated by the founders of Alcoholics Anonymous in 1939, they have become an indispensable tool for hundreds of thousands of recovering men and women. Their effectiveness has not gone unnoticed outside AA. At last count there were two hundred anonymous self-help groups that also use the steps, with only slight modifications.

The steps are *suggested* guides for recovery. There is no rule that says anyone has to do them, and there's no regulation about how they should be done. It's a matter of personal comfort and conviction, and of being continually enriched by hearing the stories of our peers.

I want to thank the young people who encouraged me to undertake this guide. With their permission, I have quoted some of the things they shared with me outside their meetings. I can assure readers that I have altered their names as well as the details of their stories to protect their anonymity.

How anonymous we are about our drinking and drugging problems is a matter of personal choice. How publicly we discuss our recovery, including our experience with the steps, is also our own decision. Actual membership in any Twelve Step fellowship, however, has to be anonymous. It's essential that we respect that anonymity for the sake of the other individuals in the fellowship and the effectiveness of the group as a whole.

STEP 1

We admitted we were powerless over alcohol—that our lives had become unmanageable. *

"How can I be an alcoholic?" fifteen-year-old Jerry asked. "I'm not even old enough to drink legally yet!"

Every young person who has ever had to confront their own alcoholism** can identify with Jerry. What may surprise young people, however, is that practically every alcoholic or

---

*The Twelve Steps are reprinted and Steps Three, Seven, and Eleven are adapted with permission of Alcoholics Anonymous World Services, Inc. Permission to reprint and adapt the Twelve Steps does not mean that AA has reviewed or approved the contents of this publication, nor that AA agrees with the views expressed herein. AA is a program of recovery from alcoholism; use of the Twelve Steps in connection with programs and activities that are patterned after AA, but that address other problems, does not imply otherwise. The original Twelve Steps of AA are reprinted in their entirety in the back of this book.
**Many young people I know are addicted to chemicals other than alcohol. Some are even addicted to behaviors, such as bulimia. For simplicity's sake only, I often refer to alcohol through much of this book. But the principles apply to any addiction, chemical or otherwise.

other drug addict, no matter what age, race or religion, sexual orientation or social background, has felt the same: addiction happens to *other* people.

No matter how strong the evidence is, we can always find a rationale to explain why we couldn't possibly be an addict or alcoholic. "My father's an alcoholic and I'm never going to be anything like *him*," runs one line of denial. "I only drink on weekends," runs another. "I'm on the honor roll!" goes a third.

If the consequences of alcoholism weren't so devastating, the excuses might be funny. But as the correlation between drugs and alcohol and teenage depression and suicide becomes clearer, the rationales grow more and more tragic. Even teenagers who are sick and tired of being told they're too young to do this or have that may be sorry to learn how democratic alcoholism is: you're *never* too young to get it.

We hear that alcoholism is a self-diagnosed disease. That can sound off-the-wall when we consider how easy it is for family, friends, teachers, and sometimes even the justice system to tell us we have a drinking and using problem. Time and time again society has tried to encourage, even force, alcoholics into sobriety. They even tried to make laws against it with Prohibition after World War I! But no matter what measures are taken, nothing will help us until we diagnose ourselves as alcoholics, admitting that we are powerless over alcohol and that alcohol has made our lives *unmanageable*.

Why the excuses? Why do we deny the problem? Are we just hopeless ne'er-do-wells who willfully refuse to see the light? If we look at ourselves in a more humane, more sympathetic way, perhaps we'll be able to see denial for what it is.

Whether or not we consciously recognize it, all of us have felt pain. Some of us grew up in homes where we witnessed and experienced abuse. For some of us, the abuse was blatant, even violent. Sometimes there was poverty as well as illness. And very often that illness was a parent's alcoholism.

▶ **You're <u>never</u> too young to get it.**

In other homes, the abuse was more subtle. There may have been money, but there was also constant complaining that it wasn't enough—or fear that it would all be gone tomorrow. Perhaps our parents treated us well enough, but we were forced to witness their cruelty to each other. Maybe our parents hurt us with expectations that we couldn't live up to.

Do alcoholics endure more pain as children than other people do? That seems unlikely. After all, pain is part of life and we *all* experience it periodically. But if you're an alcoholic

5

or other drug addict, it may well be that no one ever taught you healthy ways to handle the pain you felt. Perhaps your parents couldn't show you healthy examples because they didn't know how to handle pain themselves.

If we spoke out about our feelings, we were very often ignored. If we complained about certain abuses, we were frequently punished. It wasn't long before we learned to pretend the pain wasn't there. We began to believe that if we hid from our feelings, maybe they'd go away. This was *denial* and it was a survival technique. It helped us get through!

▶ **Denial, however, is an uphill business. The more you deny feelings, the harder it gets.**

Denial, however, is an uphill business. The more you deny feelings, the harder it gets. That's why alcohol and drugs seemed like the answer to our prayers. They seemed to take all the "work" out of ignoring our problems and hiding from our feelings. Did they make us feel more peaceful? More comfortable? More capable? Didn't booze and drugs make us feel good the first time? The second? The third? For some of us, didn't they seem to be the best fun we had going?

So what if we had been told time and time again the booze and drugs were no answer! They were better than anything else we had found. Being powerless over alcohol seemed beside the point when alcohol gave us the only power we had ever had.

For a while, a very short while, it really did feel as if life were better, more manageable than it had ever been. But then things started to sour, the denial kicked in. We told ourselves that the hangovers were a small price to pay, the problems at school really weren't that serious, the car accident would have happened even if we'd been sober.

The more we relied on drugs and alcohol, the less we depended on whatever healthy coping skills we had developed. When the troubles began, we were psychologically, if not physically, addicted to drugs and alcohol. We *believed* in drugs and alcohol and, to tell the truth, we were believing less and less in everything else.

▶ **"I kept telling myself I couldn't be an alcoholic because I never got into trouble with the law. But then I got arrested."**

Our world got smaller. Our range of options got narrower. If we admitted that our lives were unmanageable, we knew, consciously or not, that we would have to do something about our drinking and our using. But we were hooked and we couldn't look at any of that. So the solution was to insist—no matter

7

what—that our lives were manageable. How many times have we told the world, "Everything's okay. Don't worry about it"?

It became a vicious circle. We knew something was wrong. We knew it wasn't working the way it had. But we did everything we could to convince other people that *nothing* was wrong. If we didn't convince them we were okay, we convinced them that we didn't care. We pointed at other people with drinking problems. As long as there was someone else doing worse, we weren't so bad. It was insane, but it was the only way to avoid the consequences. The degree to which we kidded ourselves only goes to show how powerful the disease is—and how powerless we are over it.

"I was on the honor roll," says Liz, a seventeen-year-old high school senior who has been sober two years. "I used to point at this kid who was flunking out of school and explain *he* was an alcoholic. It protected me from dealing with the reality that I was an alcoholic too. But it didn't take long to learn that every time I point the finger at someone else, there are three other fingers pointed directly at me!"

Derek, who's sixteen, shakes his head sadly. "I was having trouble at school," he says. "But I kept telling myself I couldn't be alcoholic because I never got into trouble with the law. But then I got arrested."

"Is that when you got sober?" Jerry asks.

"No," Derek explains. "That's when I decided I couldn't be alcoholic because I wasn't sleeping in the streets."

And so it goes. The inmate doing time in prison can point to the drunk in the gutter as the *real* alcoholic, and the drunk in the gutter can point to someone else too.

▶ **It's a progressive disease. You'll hear it likened to a descending elevator.**

It wasn't very long ago that recovery from alcoholism and drug addiction was thought to be practically impossible. Even twenty years ago, a recovering alcoholic or other addict was very rare, almost exotic. Only in the last few years have we seen recovery as a normal, achievable thing.

It's a progressive disease. You'll hear it likened to a descending elevator. In the old days, alcoholics, almost without exception, went all the way to the bottom. This meant wet brain (a condition in which you lose control over your mind and body functions), institutionalization in a prison or a hospital, or even death. When AA started up, most of its members had hit bottom and had been very close to death. It was thought, mistakenly, that only drunks who had hit that bottom could take recovery seriously. Now we know

9

better. Nowadays, the elevator doesn't have to go all the way to the basement. You can push the button and get off at higher and higher floors.

But to do that, we have to start looking at ourselves. We have to stop pointing to others as the "real" alcoholics and see if we are ready for the First Step. All alcoholics and other addicts need courage for that. But the teenage alcoholic or other addict needs a little extra willingness to be honest. After all, as we get older and fall lower and lower, there just aren't as many other people to point our fingers at! Yes, young people do flunk out of school, get in trouble with the law, become depressed, and sometimes kill themselves. But there are still many, many alcoholics young people can point to and say—truthfully—that they aren't like that.

Taking the First Step means not comparing ourselves with *anybody*. It means asking ourselves honestly if we are powerless over drugs and alcohol, not if someone is more powerless than we are! It means not blaming a parent, a friend, or a teacher for our problems. It means accepting it's the alcohol and other drugs that got us into trouble. It's admitting that getting high doesn't do what it used to. It's saying we can no longer count on booze and drugs to get us "up" and "together" anymore.

What's manageable and what's unmanageable can be a very confusing question for many of us. After the troubling, almost crazy upbringing many of us have had, we get used to erratic, angry, sad, and fearful as the norm.

As Ramon, a nineteen-year-old college freshman says, "I thought everything was fine. My only trouble was I wanted to die. In my crowd that was normal. My own brother had killed himself, and we never said it had anything to do with drugs or alcohol! It was only after a whole month of sobriety that I understood that just because something's 'normal' doesn't mean it's manageable!"

The First Step has worked for thousands upon thousands of other people with addiction problems—no matter what age. But it may take a while to believe that it can work for you too! Many AAs say that it was only after they had been sober a while that they really saw just how powerless over alcohol they really were and how unmanageable life had become.

Even if you know in your heart that you are powerless over alcohol and that life has become unmanageable, you might resist taking this step. If it's because you're afraid you won't be able to make a go of sobriety, remember that you're not alone. Every recovering person, no matter what age, has felt the same. At this very moment there are untold numbers of people coming into AA feeling just as you do.

Whether it's your first day or your forty-fifth year of sobriety, it's always one day at a time. That's why so many men and women in recovery take this step again and again. Many even do it every day.

Like you, they were tentative at the beginning, but as they stayed sober, their belief in their powerlessness over alcohol and other drugs grew deeper. To their surprise, and yours too, probably, admitting they were powerless over alcohol and drugs was the first step toward finding great power within themselves.

The First Step is an invitation to a wonderful new life you may have only dreamed of. As we explore the other eleven steps, we'll learn the tools that have made that happen for thousands and thousands of recovering addicts and alcoholics.

Perhaps you're worried it's just going to get harder now. If you can admit that you are powerless over alcohol and drugs and that your drinking and drugging have made your life unmanageable, congratulations—you've just done the First Step. The hardest part is already behind you!

Come on!

STEP 2

Came to believe that a Power greater than ourselves could restore us to sanity.

"What's with this higher power stuff?" Traci, a sixteen-year-old newcomer, was saying. "I thought the only requirement for membership was a desire to stop drinking and drugging."

Jerry, sitting next to Traci, nervously bit his lip and looked worried. "AA makes you believe in God?" he asked. "Isn't that just plain undemocratic?"

The other young people in the discussion group nodded in agreement. Although the group counselor said that no one was going to be pressured into believing anything, not everyone believed her.

The counselor respected their doubts. "Would you be willing to check out the God stuff before chucking it?" she asked.

The people were skeptical—but they were willing.

The counselor pointed out that in the fifty-plus years since the steps were formulated, generation after generation of recovering alcoholics have approached the Second Step with the same doubt.

Not *everyone* with a drinking problem is skeptical about the value of a spiritual life. Many people come to the program believing God has guided them even in the worst of times. But many don't see how God could have created a world in which so many unspeakable horrors take place, seemingly on a daily basis. Finally, there are those who just don't see how it matters one way or another if there is a God.

▶ **No matter what your religious experience, Step Two makes you look at spirituality in a way you never have before.**

It might seem that Step Two will be a snap for the first group, a major hurdle for the second, and an even call for the third. The surprising fact is, however, that Step Two is a challenge for everyone. No matter what your religious experience, Step Two makes you look at spirituality in a way you never have before.

After taking this step, you may want to work toward changing your belief. You may want to leave it just where it is now. What you choose is up to you and your conscience. The key to Step Two is the willingness to look at things as openly and honestly as you can. And as with all the other steps, it's essential to remember that your best is *always* more than good enough!

If the mention of God doesn't push any buttons for you, you might be wondering just what all the fuss is about. There is a simple, honest explanation. An active spiritual life and a willingness to look at our belief system and to be open to change have proved to be crucial in helping addicts and alcoholics recover from their disease! It's a practical matter: spiritual faith *works*.

By now you've probably already heard about "the alcoholic personality." While most alcoholics and addicts become bright, witty, delightful, and incredibly charming as soon as they come into recovery, it takes a bit longer for some of the others to get it together. Now and then, you may even meet a recovering person you wouldn't want to walk down a dark alley with! As one high school senior said on her second AA anniversary, "While I love you all, I have to admit there are some of you I like a whole lot more than others!"

It's quite possible that there's no basic personality difference between alcoholics and anyone else. But it does seem that, no matter what our age, we tend to be one very, very sensitive bunch. As a group, we seem to be overly concerned, sometimes even obsessed, with finding fault and fixing blame.

Even before the evidence is in, even before we know something's gone wrong, we're the folks who seem to know for sure that we're going to get blamed for it. And most of the time, whether we admit it or not, we think we *should* be blamed for it.

Some people call it being the "piece of junk at the center of the universe." Other times it's been called "the arrogant doormat." In the AA writings, it's called "self-centered fear."

In our self-centered fear, we become the cause of everything. And because we all have a strong negative streak, we think we are the cause of everything that goes wrong—every test we fail, every disappointment, every family fight. Developing a belief in a higher power shows our willingness to consider that we are not at the core of everything. The possibility alone takes such an enormous weight off our shoulders that we decide to investigate some more. While that means even more willingness, it's well worth the effort.

How we see our higher power is, of course, a highly individual choice. Some of us find the concepts we were brought up with to be the most comfortable, the most useful. Others, particularly those of us who have not had easy, loving relationships with our family religions, often look elsewhere.

"My birth father took a hike when I was about two days old," seventeen-year-old Bill explains. "My stepfather ridiculed me because I'm gay. So the *Our Father* concept didn't work for me at all."

"In the church I went to, God was always punishing people for everything," says fourteen-year-old Ellie, who's been clean for a year now. "I didn't get sober to get punished anymore. I go out into the woods and that's where *my* higher power is. As far as I'm concerned, you don't have to belong to any religion to be deeply spiritual."

Many others in AA would agree. At the beginning of their recovery, many AAs see their home AA group as their higher power. Soon enough, however, they realize that other people really can't be their higher power. Even so, some people feel that their higher power speaks through their AA group.

▶ **"Well, you don't <u>have</u> to be crazy. But it sure helps."**

But even after we open up to the possibility that a higher power can be an effective tool, many of us do not see how the phrase "restore us to sanity" applies to us. As Jerry put it, "So I did a couple crazy things when I was drinking. Isn't it bad enough I have a drinking problem? Do I have to be crazy too?"

"Well, you don't *have* to be crazy," Bill replied. "But it sure helps."

Everyone laughed, but the group leader asked them to examine their own definitions of *insanity*. For some, insanity meant noisy, violent acting out. For others, it was going into a shell and not saying a word to a soul for days on end. As the discussion went on, it seemed everyone had a very different notion of what insanity could be.

Now that they weren't drinking and using, they didn't see themselves acting out in those "insane" ways that marked their drinking and drugging years. As far as most of them were concerned, the second half of the Second Step was probably a fine idea for *other* people.

"But what about your feelings?" the group leader asked. "What about your fears?"

"I've spent a lot of time worrying about getting into college," says Liz, who's in her last year of high school and has been sober two years. "I start worrying that my life will be over if I don't get in!"

"I get real frightened in groups," Jerry said. "Sometimes I even break out in a sweat too."

As the conversation moved around the group, almost everyone was able to admit at least one major fear that just wasn't rational. Even though the fears were all irrational, the kids admitted they had all used drugs and alcohol because of them.

"It's amazing all the crazy things I used to do," says Derek, who has been sober a year now. "Like dealing drugs behind the high school and breaking into a liquor store. I never *once* worried about the cops catching me. I've been on probation for a year now, and every day I see more clearly how really insane I was!"

Practically all the others could name similar times when they had been totally unafraid of great risks. Considering the potential consequences, it had been "insane" for them to be as fearless as they had been. Soon all but one of the teenagers saw some aspect of their present life as insane.

"Well, I can't think of one 'crazy' thing like that," said sixteen-year-old Traci. "Maybe I'm crazy not to think I'm crazy."

"How about your drinking?" asked Bill, who has been in the program two years. "Didn't you think it was going to make everything okay?"

"Sure I did," Traci admitted. "Isn't that why *everyone* drinks? Because I don't like myself too much."

"But you were getting sicker and sicker, weren't you? And you kept on drinking anyway."

"So?"

"I heard once that insanity is doing the same thing over and over and thinking the consequences are going to be different. Isn't it crazy thinking something that can kill you is going to make everything okay?"

Traci thought it over. Then she smiled. "So I'm crazy too." She laughed. "To believe all those lies booze and drugs told me, I guess I'd have to be, wouldn't I?"

Even though we like to take on too much blame, we can't take *all* the credit for not being able to tell when something's crazy and when something's not. When we took the First Step, many of us found that our upbringing had prevented us from being able to distinguish what was manageable from what was not. If we look more closely at our lives, we'll see how we learned many of our "insane" attitudes and beliefs from our families. And lest we decide to blame them for it all, let's remember that they were just passing on what they had learned from their families.

▶ **"So I'm crazy too. To believe all those lies booze and drugs told me, I guess I'd have to be, wouldn't I?"**

"We grew up not thinking very highly of ourselves because our families didn't think very highly of themselves," the group leader pointed out. "If you're open-minded, the Second Step can teach you that hating yourself is really crazy."

"In other words, the Second Step could restore me to loving myself?" Traci asked.

"That's what higher power did for me," Bill said.

Although it looks hard at first, even intimidating, generations of recovering men and women have found the Second Step is just too good an offer to refuse!

STEP 3

*Made a decision to turn our will and
our lives over to the care of God* as we
understood God.[*]

*Be still. Listen to your breathing. Let it
become deeper and more regular. Feel the tight-
ness in your muscles and bones ease a little.
Find that still, quiet place deep within you.
Touch it and feel peaceful. Remember you are
not alone.*
That's one way to do Step Three.
Help! I can't do it all by myself anymore!
That's another way.
Spend a few moments in Step Three one
morning and its warm peacefulness will stay
with you till the end of the day.
Try it another morning and it lasts only a
moment or two. It seems you're "turning it
over" every other minute.

---

[*]The change here to " . . . God as we understood God" is an
adaptation of the original Third Step of the Twelve Steps of
Alcoholics Anonymous, which reads " . . . God as we understood Him." The original Twelve Steps of AA are reprinted in
their entirety in the back of this book.

Does that mean:

A. You've lost your touch; you're probably doing something wrong (again!).
B. Your higher power has lost his/her touch (again!).
C. The Third Step is a joke.
D. Some days are the pits!

There's no right or wrong answer here. It depends on how you're feeling. Despite what many of us may have been taught, there's nothing "right" or "wrong" about feelings or about spiritual belief. Spirituality is a tool that helps some of us live happier lives. It is not a yardstick by which we measure our worth.

If you're not ready or willing, or if you're just not interested in learning how to use this particular tool, don't beat up on yourself. Whatever your reasons, they're good ones, based on real feelings that come from real experience. All you need are two things. First, a willingness to listen to other recovering people's experiences with the Third Step. And second, an openness to the possibility there may be something here for you somewhere down the line.

Of all the tools available in recovery, the Third Step has got to be the most popular. Time and time again it has helped people get through difficult moments—and helped them find solutions they never dreamed existed!

"When I got to the program, I definitely did

23

not believe in a higher power," says Derek. "I figured the Third Step didn't apply to me. It just never occurred to me that faith can start from nothing and just grow. Faith just takes time, I guess, only I didn't like *anything* that took time."

Recovering alcoholics can be as impatient as anyone else. Just like everyone else we can get frustrated when things don't happen right away. No wonder using appealed to us so much! There was no wait there. Take a pill, a hit, or a drink, and presto!—we were *there*. Process was a drag. It was for people who didn't mind wasting time. Why bother with it?

It's hard to blame anyone for wanting to feel better. Considering that fear was rampant in many of our households, we can't blame ourselves for wanting immediate relief. The problem is that booze and drugs fed our delusion that we could skip process altogether.

But like it or not, process is one of life's realities. Everything is about process, including drugs and alcohol. The more we drank, the more we needed to drink. No matter how well one drug worked, most of us wound up trying others. Even though we did our best to deny it, getting high was getting harder—and the consequences were getting more serious.

The headaches turned into monumental hangovers. The dates we missed (just because we didn't feel like it!) became more frequent. The little disagreements were becoming all-out fights. Last year's fender bender was last week's near-fatal collision. Right to the very end of our drinking and using, we denied that anything had changed—even when alcohol and drugs were threatening our lives!

So it's understandable if you don't see faith as a process either. To many of us, faith was just a black-or-white deal: some folks had it and some folks didn't. If you believed, you believed totally. If you didn't believe, you didn't believe at all. If you didn't care, you didn't care at all.

▶ **"At the beginning I felt really bad about Step Three. I mean, I'd never thought about God one way or the other and all of a sudden it's like I have to turn everything over to him."**

Some of us shied away from faith because we perceived it as something spooky and overly mystical. Many of us have been offended by the cynical, sometimes even criminal, wrongdoing and hypocrisy of certain religious leaders. To those people, it came as a real surprise that in AA one can scorn religion and still have a deep spiritual faith.

In Step Three, we learn that we don't need to believe in any religion or listen to any religious leaders in order to be spiritual. "God as we understood God" is the key phrase here and that means an unlimited freedom you may never have considered before.

At first, the freedom is a little bewildering. It may also be very confusing. That's more than okay; many of our most spiritual women and men have had profound doubts. Such doubts are part of any serious spiritual search. All that's needed in Step Three is a *willingness* to think about a higher power, find out what your feelings are, and be open to wherever your experience takes you.

"At the beginning I felt really bad about Step Three," Liz, the high school senior, admitted. "I mean, I'd never thought about God one way or the other and all of a sudden it's like I have to turn everything over to him. I just couldn't do it, and I started to worry that it was going to keep me from getting sober."

The Third Step asks us to turn our will and our lives over to the *care* of a higher power. Liz says that helped her feel more comfortable. "It just meant there was someone or something out there that was going to take care of me. In the beginning of my sobriety, there were *a lot* of things I couldn't take care of myself. Once I admitted it, working the Third Step became a real help."

Janine has been clean and sober for four years. Now nineteen, she works in a bank and is engaged to be married. She explained how her understanding of God changed in her first months of the program. "I still had my license, but I'd been in a car accident and I was really frightened about driving, especially at night. My sponsor asked if I'd try the Third Step to overcome my fear of driving. So I did, but the first time was scary and I only drove three blocks. Next time I drove a couple of miles and in a couple of weeks I was fine. That's how I've done the Third Step since then. Little by little. Block by block."

Anyone who thinks faith is blind hasn't heard how recovering people develop their own spirituality. Faith is a tool, and it's based on your own personal experience with it. As with other tools, faith gets better the more you experiment with it.

We do with faith just what we do with anything else that's new to us: we test it. If the first test goes well one day, then we'll try it again the next. Like Janine who was afraid to drive at night, we'll go a little further with it every time.

It sounds like a very slow, very laborious process. "One day at a time" can seem like forever. But if you give it a chance, you'll see how quickly those days add up.

All too often, we set our sights on the one thing, the one event, or even the one person who will make our lives work out for us. How many of us have resorted to that foxhole prayer of "God, if you'll only let me pass the test, get the job, be invited to the party, I promise I will never drink, drug, lie, cheat, steal, ask another thing of you, as long as I live!"

We become desperate. What's going to happen if the job, the grade, the date, doesn't come through? Although we may laugh at our dramatic intensity, it's important not to beat up on ourselves for it. After all, we only did what we saw others doing—especially those of us who grew up in homes where people were cold, sometimes even abusive. Our lives really did seem to be a never-ending quest for that one thing (or one person) that would make us okay, lovable, safe.

> ► **"I'm just beginning to learn that my higher power has a lot better things in store for me than I could ever imagine."**

In turning our will and our lives over to the care of a higher power, we are also turning over the outcome. As Derek says, "I'm just beginning to learn that my higher power has a lot better things in store for me than I could ever imagine." As Derek learned, insisting on one solution blinds us to other solutions that are very likely better than the ones we dreamed up.

But sad and difficult, even tragic, things *do* happen. A beloved relative dies, a friend becomes sick, a dream we were counting on

28

has to be postponed or even re-envisioned. Times like these can shake one's faith. "Is that the reward I get for being sober?" we ask. "If that's what's being handed down, I'd rather get wasted!" we conclude.

Faith does not prevent bad things from happening in our lives. But faith does help us to handle life's difficulties in better ways than we ever imagined possible. It helps us to consider a plan or purpose higher than our own. Feeling pain as we do, we can be sure that we'll get through it—and soberly too.

Pain hurts—even in sobriety. But in a very real way, it also strengthens us. We learn. We grow. As we come to understand that we were never supposed to do it alone, we accept ourselves as we are—and love ourselves better. We've asked for help and we've received it. Every time it happens, our faith grows too.

STEP 4

*Made a searching and fearless moral
inventory of ourselves.*

You won't have to go to many Twelve Step
meetings before you hear AAs fretting and
sometimes even groaning about the Fourth
Step. No step seems to arouse more anxiety
than this one. Maybe it's the prospect of being
fearless that makes us so fearful. Maybe the
word "moral" makes us dread we'll find out
that we're worse than we thought. Whatever
the reason, more than a few of us can feel for
the high school sophomore who announced,
half-jokingly, "I don't need this step! I *already*
know what a horrible person I am!"

Finding out we're worse than we ever
feared is definitely not what Step Four is
about. The *last* thing any of us needs is another chance to beat up on ourselves. Haven't
most of us been doing that long enough—all
too often with "help" from our families, teachers, and friends?

Now would be a good time to remind ourselves that the steps, like the other tools in

the program, are here to help us get more out of life, not to hurt or frighten us. If sobriety were punishment, very few people would try it in the first place, and absolutely no one would stick with it!

Remember, the only step we are asked to do perfectly is the First Step. The other steps, the Fourth included, we do as well as we can. As we do them, we learn that our best efforts, as long as we're sober and working the program, are always more than good enough.

As Ramon, who refers to himself as a "recovering garbage head" says, "From hearing the older people at the meetings, I thought it took months just to get up the courage to do it!" While some have chosen to wait a while before moving into the Fourth Step, many do their first Fourth Step within their first months of recovery. Many recovering people are introduced to the Fourth Step while they are still in rehab! On the other hand, if we just can't seem to shake the feeling that the Fourth Step is some kind of punishment, it might be a good idea to put this step off until we feel better about doing it.

Even if we're gung ho about taking on Step Four, it can be helpful to talk with our counselor or sponsor. If we're not yet comfortable staying away from drugs and alcohol one day at a time, our counselor or sponsor might suggest we keep our focus on the first three steps. Later, when we get a little more used to being drink-free and drug-free, we can tackle Step Four. If we are going through a hard time—and that's when many of us feel duty-bound to be hardest on ourselves—our counselor or sponsor might suggest that we do this step when we are being gentler with ourselves.

Even before we started using, we were already harsh in our self-assessments. Indeed, many of us have come from families that seemed to promote our low self-esteem. Our experience with others, teachers and friends included, only made us feel worse. Drinking and drugging were supposed to relieve us from that, but the more we used, the worse we felt about ourselves. Here in Step Four is our chance—for many of us our very first—to see ourselves in a kinder, sober light.

▶ **The Fourth Step is not a test. You can't fail it!**

While we may now come to grips with some character defects as well as some embarrassing and even painful memories, we need to look at the good things too. For example: Maybe we have gone to bat for friends, worked hard at school, tried hard to please our families, managed on our own in a crazy family.

Alcoholics tend to see things in terms of good and bad, right and wrong. Even before we found ourselves addicted to drugs and alcohol, we were addicted to severe judgments of everything under the sun, ourselves included! The Fourth Step gives us an opportunity to see ourselves in a light that informs but doesn't judge.

That's not to say we lose all critical judgment. In our Fourth Step, we will see some qualities as assets and others as defects. But we won't gloat over the assets as we did before, and we won't condemn ourselves because of our defects. We are sick people getting healthy, not bad people getting good.

Keep in mind that the Fourth Step is not a test. You can't fail it!

As you start your Fourth Step, spend a few minutes, maybe more if needed, going over the first three steps. Remember that admitting our powerlessness in Step One was one of the most relieving and freeing things we ever did. Remember how the Second Step helped us understand that it was crazy to think we needed to be in control. Remember that in the Third Step handing our will and our lives over to the care of a higher power gave us the greatest strength and peace we had ever known.

Now we're ready for Step Four. Set a piece of paper on a table. Put a pencil next to it. Put some food and maybe some soda or a hot drink next to it. Maybe there should be some relaxing music on the radio or CD player.

Would you be more comfortable, more in touch with yourself, outdoors? By all means, sit by a stream if that's what makes you feel good. We're here to take care of ourselves better than we ever have before, not to hurt ourselves. Remember, there's no wrong way to do this step. It's what's comfortable for us that matters!

Some of us come from abusive, even violent, households. For our Fourth Step, we have to make a special effort to keep from listing the character defects of the people who have hurt us. Although it can be a stretch, we have to keep our focus on ourselves!

▶ **If there's one thing we learn in our sobriety, it's just how fearful we've been of life.**

Being human, we are probably going to go for the "bad" qualities first, no matter how nice we try to be to ourselves. But just for once, let's give ourselves a break and try to write down some nice things. Surely we can remember more than just a few instances when we went out of our way for someone else. How about writing "helpful to others" at the top of our list? What about the times we studied hard to pass a test in order to please our parents? How about jotting down "eager to please" and "willing to work hard"? What about the time we told the truth even though we thought we could get away with a lie? How about adding "truthful" to the list?

Are you feeling uncomfortable writing down your good points? How about putting down "have trouble seeing my assets"?

Now let's see if we can look at the defects without beating up on ourselves. Perhaps we'll remember the time we snapped at someone who was only making a suggestion. Instead of saying we're just plain mean, how about jotting down "oversensitive to criticism"? What if we lied about not showing up for a date? Instead of jotting down "liar," how about jotting down "lied"? If we cheated on a test, how about jotting down "cheated" instead of "cheater"? What if we misused that wonderful sense of humor of ours and hurt someone's feelings? Instead of saying "cruel," how about writing "can be hurtful"? And what if we were sometimes careless about other people's feelings? How about jotting down "self-absorbed" instead of "doesn't care about other people"?

Let's review the list. For all the times we told lies, we have also been truthful. For all the times we have been lazy, we have also been hardworking. For all the times we have been indifferent to others, we have also been very caring about other people's welfare.

When we look over the list of "bad" things, we see the common denominator of fear behind every single one of them. How about writing down "fearful"? If you feel like it, you might want to write a list of all the things you know you're afraid of: for example, "afraid of criticism, afraid of disappointing others, afraid of not being loved, afraid of not being heard, afraid of not being fed and housed, afraid of not being safe and taken care of."

If there's one thing we learn in our sobriety, it's just how fearful we've been of life. Fear, it seems, has been our number-one character defect. As we look closer, we'll see that it is the character defect behind all our other defects.

Drugs and liquor, which we thought were going to take care of our fears forever, played a rotten trick on us. Even if we didn't seem to feel the fear (particularly at the beginning of our using), we were still acting out of that fear most of the time. No matter how much we numbed our fears, they only got worse.

Now might also be a good time to take note of some of the other things that still gnaw at us. We may remember times when we hurt people's feelings, a debt we didn't pay back, a time we were rude or even stole from someone. Just jot them down. There! It's out! And even though we feel remorseful about it, we don't feel the dread and shame that made us pretend we hadn't done those things in the first place.

Now and then, we come to a memory of something that's just too painful to handle at the current time. If that's the case, be gentle with yourself. Janine felt deeply ashamed about the way she had treated her boyfriend. At the suggestion of her sponsor, she decided to put the memory aside until she could handle it. A year later when she was a lot more comfortable with herself, she came back to it. She was able to deal with it in a highly positive, non-self-abusive manner that she wasn't up to the first time around!

Take a breath. Look over your inventory. Is there anything you'd like to add? If so, write it down. If not, why not put down the pen. Over the next day or so, you may want to add a few things, but basically, you've just finished your first Fourth Step.

Congratulations!

Remember, this is a step we can do again and again. Our next Fourth Step may be very different in form and style. The feelings may also be different. That's how we grow in our sobriety, always changing, always finding new ways that suit our individual needs.

If you have some uneasy feelings about what's come up in your inventory, you can share that at meetings. You can talk to your sponsor about it. The tools of the program are there to bring us all the peace we deserve.

For now, however, we've already made major progress. We have every reason to feel good about that. With the other steps still to do, we will continue to make more progress and feel more peace!

If we stay sober and continue to work the steps, many of our worst fears might disappear. As for the fears that don't go away, we will be handling them better than we ever could have imagined.

That's one way to do the step. It could take an hour or a whole afternoon. It might take several days. It might be pages long, but that doesn't mean it's "better" than the Fourth Step someone wrote on the back of an envelope.

As you come back to this step, you'll find ways that suit you best. The important thing now is to get started, to discover that looking into ourselves is a helpful and not a hurtful experience. For many of us, that's big news. Until we got to Step Four, our experience with introspection had been primarily masochistic. Now that we've had a positive experience with it, we can start to feel a new freedom.

It's a freeing step, the beginning of the healing that we hear so much about. Even so, most newcomers find it's the Fifth Step that brings us even greater freedom and peace.

Hang in there! It's just beginning and it only gets better!

STEP 5

Admitted to God, to ourselves, and to another human being the exact nature of our wrongs.

Peace. Relief. An incredible sense of lightness. As though a hundred-ton burden of self-centered remorse and regret had been lifted from our shoulders. But no matter how many times we hear about the benefits of Step Five, probably no one has ever approached it for the first time without dread.

"Tell someone what's wrong with me?" Ellie laughs. "In my family you didn't share *anything,* bad things especially. I learned early to tell everyone everything was okay all the time. It was the best way I knew to keep people off my back."

Bill nods in agreement. "When I said something was wrong with me, they'd say I should quit getting high. Or they'd make fun. Or they'd punish me. Or they'd blab it all over town. Talking about *anything* real wasn't a good idea around my family."

Practically all of us know how they feel. Who among us, young or old, hasn't had a bad experience sharing our honest feelings? How often have we felt safer shading and editing the truth rather than telling it like it is? How often has it felt better saying nothing at all? How can we be sure it's going to be better now—just because we're sober and following the steps?

"Trusting other people was *too* damn hard," Bill says with a sigh. "I wanted to go ask if I could get away with just telling God and myself about the exact nature of my defects. I mean two-thirds of the step is better than nothing, right?"

Maybe.

But don't count on it.

Even a relatively brief career of drinking and drugging can make an alcoholic believe all kinds of lies. We can believe that we're handling things just fine—even when everything's going down the tubes. We can believe the only damage we're doing is to ourselves—even when we're causing our families and friends real grief. We can promise we're going to quit one minute, and get our hands on a six-pack the next.

Even if we have knowingly lied to someone else, we never *mean* to lie to ourselves. Most of us think we're rigorously honest with ourselves, probably because we tend to confuse rigorous honesty with self-abuse! But the fact is this: Our ability to fool ourselves is limitless when we're talking only to ourselves.

40

That is why the role of another person in Step Five is essential. If we're not telling it to another person, we have no reality check.

Even before finishing the Fourth Step, you will probably be considering how to go about doing the Fifth. Most likely, your thoughts will center on the people you are going to do your Fifth Step with. Can you trust them to listen sympathetically? Can you be sure they won't judge or criticize you as others have in the past? How can you know they'll still like you after you've finished telling them things you never dared tell anyone else before?

▶ **Our ability to fool ourselves is limitless when we're talking only to ourselves.**

Almost always, people ask their sponsor to hear their Fifth Step. That's someone with whom you already have an ongoing relationship. In your dealings with sponsors, you have already found them to be supportive, sympathetic, and trustworthy. You already know that they're in your corner and know just where you are coming from. As you start, you know that whatever anxiety you may feel is more about breaking your vow of secrecy than about any reservations you might have about them!

"I was worried about what my sponsor would think when she found out I'd gotten pregnant my first year in junior high," Ellie says. "My voice was shaking when I told her. When she started to cry a little, I got really worried until she explained she felt so bad for the pain and shame I'd been through. I cried too that someone cared about me that much. I never felt so close to another human being before."

You may feel that your sponsor is not the ideal person to hear your Fifth Step. If, for instance, your sponsor happens to be struggling with anger over a recent mugging, you might understandably feel wary of confiding that one of your major wrongs was an act of theft.

Those fears are rarely justified—but if they're holding you back from taking the Fifth Step, it's a good idea to search out someone else. (If you would like to share most of your Fifth Step with your sponsor, but prefer to share the rest of it with someone else, why not consider that possibility?)

Let's remember that not everybody has a sponsor. Nor do we all have a good rapport with our sponsor. If for some reason you're not able to find another sponsor, by all means find someone else to talk to.

Generally speaking, of course, it's easier to go to people in the fellowship. After all, they did their Fifth Step for the first time once too and they know how you're feeling. But if you feel more comfortable with someone outside the program, why not ask that person to hear you?

Some prefer to do their Fifth Step with a family minister, priest, or rabbi. For very good reasons, some feel safer doing it with a minister, priest, or rabbi their family has never met.

Some even prefer to do their Fifth Step with someone they've met only briefly and will never run into again.

▶ **"It's easy now doing the Fifth Step. But the first time I didn't know if I was going to make it through, I was so nervous."**

As Bill says, "At my home group, even with my sponsor, I couldn't stop worrying they were going to judge me for being gay just like my stepfather did. I was afraid they'd think it was one of my defects, and that's not how it is for me at all. So I went to a gay men's meeting a hundred miles from home and asked a guy there if I could do my Fifth Step with him. He said it would be okay. So a couple days later I spoke to him for about an hour at a diner. I never ran into him again, but I'll always be grateful. I knew that doing the steps was keeping me sober, but if I couldn't have done it the way I did, I probably wouldn't have done it period. Afterwards, I told my sponsor and some of the people in my group, and they were cool about it. It was nice to know my fears about them had been groundless. But in order to tell them, I needed to tell that guy a hundred miles away first."

Janine also did her Fifth Step with someone other than her sponsor. "I knew it was the right thing for me on account of my background being so really different from my sponsor's, but I thought she'd feel bad about it so I didn't tell her," Janine explains. "But then I started feeling guilty, so I did tell even though I worried she was going to fire me. She was really nice and really sorry I was so upset. She said my Fifth Step was for me, not for anyone else, her included. I know that's what sobriety is all about. But after not taking care of *me* all my life, it's hard to remember that sometimes."

Ramon, who's had over five years in the program, adds, "It's easy now doing the Fifth Step. But the first time I didn't know if I was going to make it through, I was so nervous. Instead of taking it one day at a time, I did it one moment at a time. I decided that if I got to feeling weird during the thing, I could just stop before I got to the really gruesome parts. When we started, I thought I wouldn't be able to say one word. A couple minutes into it, I knew I could say anything and it would be okay. Since then it's hard to shut me up!"

Ideally, make a date when both of you are likely to be as refreshed and alert as possible. Pick a time when nothing major is looming either immediately before or immediately after.

It's also good to pick a spot that will be comfortable for both parties, a place where there will be no (or at least very few) interruptions.

If the person with whom you are doing your Fifth Step suggests his or her home and you feel more comfortable in your own home, don't hesitate to say so! If you're fresher in the morning, suggest you meet after breakfast on the weekend. As Janine points out, the Fifth Step is for you. Taking an active role in picking someone to do it with, picking the spot and the time, will help you feel considerably less fearful.

▶ *"I kind of figured I was the worst kid who ever lived. To tell you the truth, I was disappointed to find out my sponsor had been worse!"*

Most people come to the Fifth Step meeting with their Fourth Step in hand. They refer to the inventory rather than read it aloud. If you like, feel free to speak about certain areas of your life in more depth. Don't worry about how it comes out. Neatness doesn't count!

We might start with a couple of character defects that we're not too proud of. We might move on to some feelings we're uncomfortable with. We may also speak about experiences—things we did or things that were done to us—that we never told another soul about.

45

Almost invariably, we are surprised at and relieved by the response. Usually, our listeners identify with practically every feeling we've ever had. Often they can also mention some incident from their past to show us that they have had comparable, if not identical, experiences. "I kind of figured I was the worst kid who ever lived," Janine says, laughing at the memory of her first Fifth Step. "To tell you the truth, I was disappointed to find out my sponsor had been worse!"

In a very real way, Step Five is a step out of our isolation. For too long we have been afflicted with terminal uniqueness. No matter what other people said they felt, not one of them had ever felt as bad, as sad, as put upon, as ashamed, as embarrassed, as we did. No one in the world could ever feel as all alone or as "different" as we did.

But in talking more openly about ourselves, we invite people to talk more openly about themselves too. The more we hear, the more we realize that we aren't so different from other people. They may look very different and their experiences may be very different too. But at the core, people really feel all the same things.

As you come to the end, the person with whom you have done your Fifth Step may point out that you mentioned only defects and no assets. You're likely to remind him or her that Step Five calls for "the exact nature of our wrongs" only. You'll be right (on a technicality), but don't ignore the point. Being sober means remembering our assets too. For most of us, that takes discipline, even vigilance. But it's what keeps us sober and makes our lives richer and happier.

Like most of us, you'll probably feel relief that the Fifth Step is finally over. You'll very likely feel connected and very light too. As the days go by, you may feel even more benefits.

Ellie says, "I felt like I was *in* AA after I'd done my Fifth. It felt like I really belonged. The next time I went to a Fourth Step or Fifth Step meeting, I put in my two cents and a newcomer said it really helped and I could hardly believe it. I thought it would be a million years before I could help anyone else, and I'd only been in the program three months!"

"I felt it was like learning to talk all over again," Bill adds. "Before, I was always saying something to get something. I wanted to make people laugh, or I wanted them to say I was okay. And sometimes, with my stepfather, I just wanted him to feel real guilty. But when I was doing the Fifth Step, I just talked to get things off my chest. Now I see that they call it 'sharing' because that's really what it is."

Ramon says, "Before I did the Fifth Step, I always thought my defects were what hurt other people. It never occurred to me that my defects hurt me a lot too. When I finished the

Fifth Step, it was the first time I was really glad there were more steps. Well, *kind* of glad," he adds with a laugh.

As our addiction progressed, we grew wearier and warier of others. It seemed to us that people were obstacles in our path to happiness. As far as we were concerned, life would be a whole lot simpler, and often a whole lot safer, if there just weren't other people to deal with.

In Step Five, we begin to turn that around. For many of us, it's the most positive experience we have had with another human being in a long, long time. It is a new beginning in trusting and caring. Many of us have come away from Step Five, recognizing that it is through knowing other people that we begin to know ourselves and our higher power better.

STEP 6

*Were entirely ready to have God
remove all these defects of character.*

Character defects don't disappear into thin
air just because we quit using.

But sometimes that seems to be exactly
what happens.

Did we ever con bartenders and liquor store
owners with phony IDs? Did we steal booze
from our parents or our friends' parents? Or
lie about where we were the night before?
How about those lame excuses we tossed off
on teachers and bosses? Now that we're sober,
we don't need to do any of that anymore.

As our self-confidence emerges, we're
more comfortable with ourselves. That makes
it easier to be with other people too. We're no
longer falling back on the tired old put-downs,
the not-so-nice jokes (which weren't so funny
either), the endless secrets, the terrible
silences and angry outbursts that kept friends
and family at a distance. We're more responsible with money too.

By the end of our first ninety days, people are noticing how much better we are. When they compliment us on our progress, we don't tell them they're jerks either. Wow! If we can just hang in there another ninety days, we'll be practically perfect.

As we move in on the Sixth Step, we may wonder if it's really necessary. After all, won't the rest of our defects go away in time? Isn't fretting over our defects the kind of negative thinking that we're supposed to be growing away from now? Aren't we supposed to look at the glass as half full now, rather than half empty?

So why bother with Step Six?

1. Because sobriety has left us with too much free time and we need to find a way to kill it.
2. Because talking about our defects has recently become very fashionable.
3. Because our sobriety depends on it.

This time, the *only* answer is number 3.

Nothing, not even our recovery, can stand still. Without continually working on ourselves, we start to lose the benefits we have reaped in our recovery. Step Six helps us keep the focus on ourselves. It encourages us to stay open-minded to the chances for more self-improvement. Step Six helps guarantee, one day at a time, that sense of accomplishment and personal freedom we are beginning to love. By helping us look squarely at our defects so we can become ready to let them go, Step Six also brings us one step closer to knowing and trusting our higher power.

As we begin Step Six it's a good idea to see how far we have already come. We've admitted our powerlessness in the First Step. Then in the Second we've recognized the insanity of our former way of life, and in the Third we've made a decision to turn our will and our lives over to the care of a higher power of our own understanding. In the Fourth Step we've made an inventory of ourselves, and in the Fifth Step we've shared feelings and experiences we thought we'd never share with another soul.

> ▶ **Nothing, not even our recovery, can stand still. Without continually working on ourselves, we start to lose the benefits we have reaped in our recovery.**

As anyone, young or old, can tell you, every step represents a way of thinking and acting that is radically different from anything we have ever done before. Keeping that in mind helps prepare us for the major changes that occur with the Sixth and Seventh Steps. But even with five major steps behind us now, the Sixth Step can feel more like a leap than a step.

Liz, the high school senior, says, "My sponsor was guiding me through the steps on a very regular basis. I was doing almost one a month. I was liking them okay and I was feeling good about myself too. But when I got to the Sixth Step, I just kind of slowed down. And after three months, I realized I had totally stopped. It was a tough step for me. I just couldn't believe that all my character defects would go just like that. I had to learn that the only step we need to do perfectly is the First. The other steps we just do our best with. Not beating up on myself (again!) for not being perfect was major progress for me."

Ramon adds, "It's one thing to say something's a defect. It's another thing to mean it from your heart. In order to do the Sixth Step, I had to learn the difference between the two."

Liz nods in agreement. "Take my drinking. There was a time *everyone,* my mom especially, thought my drinking was a defect. She told me often enough, but it didn't get me sober. It only made me lie and be defensive and keep secrets. I didn't get sober because my mom had a problem with my drinking. I didn't come into the program until I decided *I* had a drinking problem!"

Many seek treatment because of pressure from families, friends, and employers. Some come to AA because of intervention by the legal system. But no one *stays* in recovery because of outside pressure.

Even when we knew intellectually that our using wasn't good for us, we still thought it was the best way we knew to get any peace.

"When I started drinking, I thought it was the best thing that ever happened to me," Ramon states. "It was killing me, but I didn't know how to live without it. It was crazy, but I really thought it was an asset until the very end! That's the way it is with all my other character defects. Way down deep, if I'm honest, I kind of think they're assets too."

If we don't honestly see a character trait as a defect, we are not going to be ready to let anyone, even a higher power, remove it.

▶ **All the emotions are gifts from a higher power and all have positive uses.**

The first defects that we see as defects— and the easiest to give up—are the ones that have hurt other people. Even defects as serious as lying, cheating, and stealing are easy to get rid of once we see there is no advantage in having them—even when we believe we can get away with them. Unless it becomes necessary to steal again in order to survive, like the homeless boy who must steal bread to eat, we will never do that again.

As we move along, however, we come to see defects that are not so easily relinquished. We also see some defects that we never knew existed before. At first this can be downright discouraging. It *feels* as though we've taken a step backwards, as though we're getting worse. But to the recovering alcoholic, this is really a sign that another weight will soon be lifted from our shoulders. Even if you have been in recovery only a short while, you'll know that every step pays dividends far in excess of the effort invested in it.

Let's say we have a tendency to be overcritical of people. That's a defect by just about anyone's standards. But as we look more closely at it, we may see that putting others down has kept us from seeing how very bad we feel about ourselves. Now that we're sober and liking ourselves better, we don't "need" that defect the way we used to.

So in the Sixth Step, we can become ready and willing to let that go. If and when we do slip back into our old behavior, we'll be quick to see it's really about low self-esteem. We can talk about it at meetings and with our sponsor. We can see that others have handled the same problem and solved it too. Whatever remains of that defect becomes an opportunity for greater self-awareness and growth.

What about anger? On the surface, it sounds wonderful to be rid of that defect once and for all. But when we look more closely at our family life, we may discover that our anger is a major survival tool. We have to remember that *all* the emotions are gifts from a higher power and that they all have positive uses. When expressed appropriately, anger can give us the bolt of energy we need to save our necks. If our anger served to get us out of frightening situations, if it served to scare dangerous people away from us, then it can hardly be a defect.

In alcoholic or other troubled households, however, anger seems to be the all-purpose emotion, no matter what the occasion. To be without anger, even inappropriate anger, could have made home life even more unsafe for us. But we used anger badly with friends, with teachers, with co-workers, and even with bosses.

Now that we're sober we can see the harm our anger does us. Does that mean we should be entirely ready to give up our anger? Hardly! There are times when anger will be a real asset. So it's not anger that we want removed. It's *inappropriate*, "self-justified" anger we want lifted.

Let's move on to the much-talked-about "trust issues." Time and time again you'll hear how hard it is for alcoholics to trust— and how vital it is to change.

Yet more often than not, *not trusting* was a saving grace for many of us in the past. How many of us have felt let down because a parent failed to prove trustworthy? In many of our families, there may have been reason to distrust that even basic needs of food, shelter, and clothing would be provided in a regular, dependable way.

Even when material needs were met, how often did we find that our emotional needs were not? Some of us experienced excessive heaps of love one day, only to find it totally gone the next. How many of us never received love at all? In learning not to trust that others would provide for us, we were taking remarkably good care of ourselves.

In sobriety we learn that it doesn't have to be that way anymore. You can make choices about the world you live in and the people you work with and play and live with. You can make a choice about your family, adopting your Twelve Step friends as your new family. You can trust others because you can trust yourself, your judgment, and your higher power. So when you do the Sixth Step, become willing to give up inappropriate distrust as well as inappropriate trust.

Remember that our so-called defects didn't come from nowhere. But now that we are different, our needs are different. The Sixth Step helps us prepare to take an active role in this new, healthier world we are now a part of! It's another step toward reconciling our new selves with that new world.

Ramon explains it this way: "When I was a newcomer, I had to rely on everyone else's experience, strength, and hope to get an idea of what the program had to offer. My recovery was what I had heard about from everyone else. It was when I got to the Sixth Step, when I started working on my own defects, that I saw my recovery wasn't going to look like anyone else's. I wasn't unique but I was more like my own man now."

Even with all the preparation you are doing in the Sixth Step, you probably still have serious reservations. You might be asking yourself, *Can I let go of some of my most monumental defects?* even after you know there's no benefit to them anymore.

That's why we have the Seventh Step. It's there that we see God doing for us what we really could not do for ourselves! For many of us, it's the miracle that turns doubters into believers.

STEP 7

Humbly asked God* to remove our shortcomings.

As Ellie, who has been in recovery from her marijuana addiction for a year, says, "Even when I was a real little kid, no matter how nice I asked, my mom always got mad. I learned early on not to ask *anyone* for *anything*. God included."

"Oh, I was *always* asking for something," Derek admits. " 'Get me out of this jam,' mostly. It's what they call 'foxhole praying.' But I guess desperate isn't the same as humble, is it?"

He adds, smiling now at the memory, "I was always asking for *other* people's defects to be removed, and right away. I don't know why it never occurred to me to ask for God to remove my own. It's not as though I didn't think I had any."

---

*The change here to "Humbly asked God . . ." is an adaptation of the original Seventh Step of the Twelve Steps of Alcoholics Anonymous, which reads "Humbly asked Him . . ." The original Twelve Steps of Alcoholics Anonymous are reprinted in their entirety at the back of this book.

Again, it's a matter of what we were brought up to believe. Perhaps we saw our family going from bad to worse. Maybe our dealings with friends only grew more difficult. Or we struggled with learning disabilities, or our schoolwork deteriorated. These experiences make it a challenge to believe that anything, including the Seventh Step, can make our lives better.

Many of us saw our parents blaming everyone else for their problems, sometimes even *us*. Following their example, we too blamed our teachers, our friends, and our families. We blamed ourselves for not being bright enough, or attractive enough, or nice enough. No one showed us how looking into ourselves, identifying a defect, and then working on it could turn everything around.

Admitting that you had a problem, expressing a sincere desire to change, and asking for help—because you knew gut-level you couldn't do it all by yourself—were the first steps that began to turn that around. From the beginning you could see things were getting better. But always you must be mindful that the big change started within you, with your willingness to change. If the world around us, our school, our friends, our family, are ever going to be better, *we* have to get better first.

It means recognizing our pessimistic attitudes and daring to be optimistic. Certainly, our dependence on outside things to make us feel good suggests we don't believe we have what it takes. Even when we cease to believe in the drink and the drug, we still look to other outside things to make us like ourselves.

We need good grades to tell us we're smart. We need good clothes to tell us we're attractive. We need a paycheck to tell us our work is worthwhile. We need certain friends to make sure we feel likeable, and we need a relationship to tell us we're loveable. While almost anybody would like all of these things, it's pessimists who *need* it to feel good about themselves. It's pessimists who fall apart when any of these friends or the special relationship is lost.

▶ "My negativity, it was like insurance. When things didn't work out, it didn't hurt so much if I'd kind of expected it. The trouble was that it wasn't going to get better till I dared to hope."

While alcoholics and addicts are really no more pessimistic than anyone else on the face of the earth, we seem to be the ones who get into the most trouble without negative attitudes. If someone else gets depressed, that person lives through it. If we get depressed, we use chemicals—and our chances of surviving our depression grow slimmer each time.

No matter how high our most recent bottom was, there's no guarantee that our next binge won't result in death.

But even when we stop denying the dire consequences of our negativism, even when we acknowledge that it really is a life-and-death issue, we *still* have trouble trying to be positive.

Janine explains it this way: "My negativity, it was like insurance. When things didn't work out, it didn't hurt so much if I'd kind of expected it. The trouble was that it wasn't going to get better till I dared to hope."

"When I came into the program, I didn't see how I was negative," Bill says. "I was like the class clown, always joking about everything. Even though I drank and drugged, I thought I was a very optimistic person. Now I see that clowning was my way of getting attention. I didn't think other people would like me if they knew who I really was. But when I started working this step and asking higher power to take away what was making me clown it up, right away I started feeling a lot better. So I really am glad I'm on to myself now."

One aspect of negative thinking is feeling sure you're not going to get what you need in life. Janine says, "After a while of not getting what I asked for, I stopped asking. If I could get something without too much trouble, it was okay. But trying was too painful. It felt safer not asking."

So if you're feeling wary of just asking, you're not alone. Just about everyone who has walked into a Twelve Step program has felt the same way. Asking God can make it even more difficult. Many of us have been too incredulous about the existence of a god even to bother to carry on a conversation with a higher power. Others have asked and been disappointed too often to risk being disappointed again. Besides, aren't we supposed to remove our personality defects by sheer willpower?

▶ **"The hardest thing for me was enabling my mom's drinking. . . . She got tight a lot of nights, and in the morning I'd have to call her boss and say she had the flu."**

"Ever since I got sober, I've been hearing and thinking a lot about higher power," Derek says. "I did the steps to the best of my ability, but I didn't have a very personal relationship with God. I'd hear God loves alcoholics so I figured he loved me too. That kind of thing. It was in Step Seven when I knew I needed a higher power who could deal with my own special stuff. It's where I got a personal relationship with my higher power."

"It always seemed like I liked my friends better than they liked me," Liz says. "That changed a lot when I got to AA, but I still kept being attracted to unavailable guys. I didn't know the name for that character shortcoming, but I knew I wanted to get rid of it. So I prayed for God to remove whatever it was that got me hooked on guys who weren't hooked on me. I'd never done the Seventh Step. It felt like I was taking a big risk until I realized I really didn't have anything to lose."

Bill says, "The hardest thing for me was enabling my mom's drinking. She kept saying it was okay for her to drink because she didn't have a problem. But she got tight a lot of nights, and in the morning I'd have to call her boss and say she had the flu. It was hard on my sobriety, but to tell you the truth I was afraid not to enable her. So I asked higher power to take away my fear. It worked too. My mom was really pissed at me. When I wouldn't call her boss for her, she said I wasn't being respectful. But doing the Seventh Step let me see that I *was* being a good son, even if my mom didn't exactly appreciate it."

The work we do in the Seventh Step has taken considerable time and effort. It began with our Fourth Step work and continued through our Fifth and Sixth Step work. Therefore, when we ask our higher power to remove a shortcoming, it's not a decision we have arrived at lightly or on the spur of the moment. We have gone through the process of recognizing a defect, examining it, and sharing about it. When we reach the Seventh Step we know in our hearts that we want that shortcoming to be removed—and we also know that only a power greater than ourselves can take it from us.

"I've been in therapy almost all my life," Liz says. "Okay, only a couple of years, but it feels like most of my life. And all the time I kept thinking that therapy would do it. I didn't do the Fourth and Fifth Steps because I figured I was already doing a Fourth Step with my therapist. I didn't do the Sixth or Seventh Steps either because I figured if you talked about the character defect enough, it would just go away.

"I had a big problem with screwing up," she continues. "Every time I'd get close to something working out, I'd do something to make it go bad. My therapist and I talked about it for a year. When it didn't go away, I got hopeless because I had all these friends in the program who were turning things around and I wasn't. When I did the Sixth and Seventh Steps, it was a last-ditch effort, believe me. I didn't have all that much faith, just a little, but it took. Now when I get to one of those places where I screw up, I ask higher power to take care of me and she does. It's been two years since I sabotaged myself. I still go to therapy, but now I use the steps too!"

It's a national disgrace that so many teenagers like Liz had to learn so much about self-sufficiency at such a young age. Because many of us had too little support at home, we came to believe that if we couldn't take care of things ourselves, no one could. While that belief helped us avoid the constant pitfall of asking for help and guidance from people who could offer neither, it also encouraged a major defect of *arrogance*.

▶ **"Doing anything humbly just wasn't my style."**

One form of arrogance is that we consider our problems worse than anyone else's. Another is that we consider our problems unique. Both of these forms effectively remove us from identifying with members of the human race. A third form is that no one and no thing can possibly take care of someone with our problems and the terrible feelings we have. Without even knowing it, we have made ourselves our own higher power.

It's an obstacle every alcoholic and addict faces, and it's why the key opening word in the Seventh Step is "humbly."

Ramon says, "Doing anything humbly just wasn't my style. I'd seen my dad act like that and it never got him anything good. It was my sponsor who taught me there was a lot of difference between being humble and groveling like my dad used to do."

Haven't we all at some time considered "humility" as a form of self-abasement? In recovery, however, we learn that the word has a very different meaning.

" 'Humble' means seeing things as they really are," Ramon adds. "It means that I'm not God. It means I can't do it by myself. My friends are terrific, but they can't fix me either. Only God can do that. He's what makes the whole miracle happen."

STEP 8

Made a list of all persons we had harmed, and became willing to make amends to them all.

Until you are at peace with your past, you cannot find peace in the present or look hopefully to the future. If you've thought there's nothing you can do about the past, you're in for a surprise. While no one can rewrite history, there are very real efforts we can make to correct it.

Step Eight is the way out of the remorse and regret that can plague our lives and threaten our chances for long-term sobriety. It is the step we use to own up to and correct the mishaps and misdeeds of our past. It frees us once and for all from the "woulda-coulda-shoulda" syndrome that holds us hostage to our worst feelings about ourselves. Once we have done it, we are well on our way to being free from that sense of impending doom many drug addicts and alcoholics have felt all their lives.

But even with that bright promise, the prospect of doing Step Eight makes first-timers uneasy. "I got nervous because I lumped Step Eight with Step Nine," says Derek. "But it was only *after* I made up the list and showed it to my sponsor that I really understood the difference between the two steps. I thought I had to make an amends to everyone on my list right away. I got so frightened about it that I stopped making up the list. When I went over it with my sponsor, he explained that making the amends is Ninth Step stuff. One step at a time, remember?

"After Step Five, I figured I wouldn't need my sponsor so much," Derek says. "But when I got to Eight, I found out I needed him more. I guess the humility around here never stops!"

If we have done our Fifth Step with our sponsors, they will already know about many of our misdeeds. If we share our lists with them, we can get help and insight. Perhaps a sponsor will suggest that we are taking on too much responsibility. Perhaps a sponsor will say that some items should be tabled for further investigation at a later date when the situation is clearer. A sponsor may even point out that we are the ones who should be receiving amends rather than owing one!

"Considering I've been saying 'I'm sorry' *all* my life, this step should have been a snap!" nineteen-year-old Janine laughs. "It took me a while to get that it wasn't just another chance to beat up on myself."

"I knew there were people I hurt," Ellie admits sadly. "My folks especially. Just thinking about it made me feel bad and guilty. My sponsor suggested that I wasn't ready. A couple months later, I came back to the step. I was ready then. To tell you the truth, I was glad I waited."

▶ **Only someone who feels worthless would try so hard to be the cutest kid, the class brain, the best athlete, or the meanest, laziest, rottenest kid in town.**

For anyone who has done Step Eight, it means the beginning of a comfort with people, a comfort that we have never experienced before. But until we have done it, we can only take other people's word for it. Keeping in mind that the steps are here to guide us gently and lovingly on our journey, we may need to edge our way surely but slowly into making a list of people whom we have harmed.

Understandably, the very notion of acknowledging our responsibility for hurting others can shake us up. It may seem more like punishment for our "sins" than freedom from the guilt and shame that we have felt about our wrongdoing.

Let's not push ourselves into unloving, self-abusive spaces that undermine our sobriety with this step. Let's dig as deep as we can—without hurting ourselves. After we have had some experience with this step and personally know its benefits, we can do our digging with lighter hearts.

We can work Step Eight most effectively if we approach it with a clear picture of who we are. For most of us, our addiction brought us *and* our self-esteem to an all-time low. The sorry fact is that many addicts and alcoholics have suffered from a poor self-image most of their lives.

One aspect of low self-esteem is our belief that we have little, if any, effect on other people. Considering the sometimes outrageous things we've done to attract attention, that may be hard to see at first. But if we look closer into human nature, we see that only someone who feels worthless would try so hard to be the cutest kid, the class brain, the best athlete, or the meanest, laziest, rottenest kid in town.

In working up our list, in looking at the effect we have on other people, we begin to see, perhaps for the first time, that we really aren't invisible. We see that people have cared about us, and loved us, and all too often worried about us too.

Another point to keep in mind is the confusion about responsibility that appears over and over again in the alcoholic family. All too often, we have grown up believing we are responsible for things beyond our control. This belief kept us distracted from the things we really *could* control. The last line of the Serenity Prayer, in which we ask for the wisdom to know the difference between what we can change and what we can't, reflects our desire to grow out of that confusion. The Eighth Step is a major action toward just that end.

As with so many of the steps, this one loses its fearsome power once we settle down to do it. Perhaps the clearest, least complicated amends have to do with money. Are there people from whom we have borrowed money and not been able to pay it back? Are there people we stole from while we were drinking? How or when we will pay them back isn't the issue now. We'll deal with it when we get to Step Nine. For now, just write down their names.

While we cannot accept responsibility *for* other people, we need to accept our responsibility *to* other people. At one time or another, practically all of us have put our alcoholism or drug addiction ahead of other people's welfare. In order to get our booze and our drugs, we have resorted to behavior we would never have considered if we had been clean.

Did we lie to our families? Did we make them worry? Did we make promises to take

71

care of problems (our drinking and drugging included) that we never made good on?

Are there brothers and sisters whom we were rude to or impatient or secretive with? How about grandparents who deserved more respect? How about a pet that deserved better care? Were there teachers we tried to con and stall?

Did we ever try to take credit that was due someone else?

Were we sometimes less than respectful of other people's feelings—and their rights? Did we bully people? Did we physically or verbally threaten people? If they had (or still have) a problem with drugs and alcohol, that doesn't mean we don't owe them amends for our wrongdoing.

▶ **"I figured I didn't owe <u>anybody</u> amends. They were all screwed up and anything I did to them, they done to me twice over and worse."**

Let's remember that booze and drugs can lead even young people into the most serious crimes there are. Did we steal from other people or vandalize their property? Did anyone get hurt in a fight with us? Did anyone die?

"I figured I didn't owe *anybody* amends," Liz says. "They were all screwed up and anything

I did to them, they done to me twice over and worse. But my sponsor said even if you don't ever intend to make amends to them, you should put them on your list."

"I wouldn't put my stepfather on the list," Bill says. "He was a creep and he was always causing my mom grief and he didn't deserve amends. It wasn't till my third time around with this step that I understood putting him on the list was more for me than it was for him. I don't feel bad that I didn't do it the first time. I mean, if you're not sincere, there's no point to it. Besides, the program's about progress, not perfection."

Liz agrees. "The first time I went through the steps, I wanted to be the best little sober person in the world and I wanted my sponsor to like me better than all her other sponsees. So I just couldn't put enough people on my list. My sponsor told me there wasn't any point to go to the top of the class on account of nobody ever graduates. After that, I started to take it easier."

Working the Eighth Step also helps us see relationships in a different light. "I used to think being in the clear legally was all it took," Bill explains. "I'd never broken the law, so I thought I didn't have to put anyone on my list. But there were things, like the way I always undervalued my sister and let her know in one way or another that she didn't count. It wasn't anything illegal and it was nothing immoral either. But I shouldn't go around telling people they don't count, because I know how bad it feels when people make me feel that way."

"When I got into the program, I started feeling bad about all the kids I had sold drugs to," Derek says. "I didn't know their names and I didn't know where most of them were anymore, but I had to put them on my list. I also stole. Even though I was arrested and on probation for it, I still had to put the owner of the liquor store I robbed on my list."

"I stole too, but from my family," Janine says. "I figured I didn't have to put them on my list because *everybody* in my family stole. If one of us saw something we wanted, we just took it. We never lied about it either. I mean, we were shameless. I got sober before anyone else in my family got into the program. So I figured why make amends to any of them? They're still going to keep on stealing from me, aren't they? But I did the amends anyway, and it was funny because it was the first time anyone in my family had ever said that it's not okay to steal. It's lucky I did this step *before* I went to work in a bank," she adds with a laugh. "I don't think the depositors would like me so much the way I used to be!"

When we say out loud that certain behaviors are unacceptable and that we will never behave that way again, we are also stating that we will not accept that kind of behavior from others. Like all the other steps, Step Eight opens the way for a new freedom most of us have never before experienced.

STEP 9

*Made direct amends to such people
wherever possible, except when to do
so would injure them or others.*

How many of us have dreamed of being free
from our fear of other people . . . free from our
fear of financial insecurity . . . free from feeling
helpless too much of the time.

If you've been into drugs and alcohol and
suffered the consequences of your addiction,
you may have forgotten that life really can be
joyous and free. If you grew up in a household
where there was alcoholism or drug abuse,
you might have never even imagined it.

But those are just three of the AA
Promises. If you don't know about the promises yet, don't let another day pass without
checking them out. If you haven't seen them
posted on the walls in the meeting rooms or
heard them read aloud, they're on pages 83-
84 of the Big Book (third edition), in the
chapter called "Into Action."*

---

*The AA Promises are reprinted at the back of this book.

"I heard the promises lots of times," says Janine. "I figured they were bull like every other promise I ever heard. But so far everyone who stays sober and works the program says the promises are for real. Fifty years and no one's said they don't work, which was proof enough, even for me."

To the thousands and thousands of recovering people who experience the promises working in their lives one day at a time, it's no surprise that the promises come right after the essay on Step Nine. Time and again, recovering men and women in Twelve Step programs have reported that the promises begin to come true *after* they make their amends.

The peace we were grateful to feel now and then becomes an almost everyday experience. The inner confidence we thought belonged only to other people becomes our own. We're handling people and situations that paralyzed us before—and we're handling them with hardly any struggle at all! Real friends, a happy capital *R* Relationship, better grades, more success on the job—and better pay to show for it too . . . the things we thought could never be ours are now within our grasp if we're willing to work for them. It all begins the day we put down the drink and the drug. But it's amazing how doing the Ninth Step moves our lives into high gear.

While no one will ever totally explain all the miracles of sobriety, there's no great mystery as to why the Ninth Step is key in making the promises come true in our lives. As long as we haven't tried to correct our misdeeds, we will expect (very often unconsciously) some kind of retribution—divine or otherwise. As long as we are reluctant to give up the defects that compelled us to commit those errors, we will never be free to let the promises work in our lives.

If, for instance, we have stolen and not made our amends for it, we will suspect that others will steal from us. If someone does steal from us, we will feel that somehow we deserved it. If we lie, we will worry other people are lying. No matter how self-righteous we are in our anger about other people's behavior, we will sense deep down that we deserved it.

Call it karmic energy or cosmic justice, but until we change our ways, we will be easy prey. If we are treating other people badly, we are in effect saying that we believe we should be treated unfairly too. What we do to others is what, unconsciously, we're asking others to do to us. Do we really want to feel this way all the time?

If, however, we have changed our ways, if we treat people honestly and honorably, we will be more likely to attract only people who treat us honestly and honorably too. When now and then a creep does mess around with us, we know how to handle the situation with minimum damage to ourselves.

"I used to gossip," Liz admits, "and believe me it wasn't pretty. You can also believe that when people gossiped about me, it really hurt me and got me angry. I mean, who can defend themselves against gossip? Besides, in an anonymous program like AA, gossip can really hurt people. I wanted everyone else to change. Only they didn't. So that's when I changed. I realized I hurt people with my gossip, and I decided not to do that anymore. Nowadays, I really don't think people gossip about me. And now and then when someone does, it just doesn't get to me. Because I'm not doing anything to deserve it, is why!"

▶   **"I wanted everyone else to change. Only they didn't. So that's when I changed."**

As Bill explained it to one of his sponsees, "You know that old 'God will get you' stuff? Well, I always *knew* something or someone was going to get me for the things I wasn't too proud of. But once I'd made my amends, I didn't have to worry about any of that stuff. Thanks to the Ninth Step, I feel I deserve a lot better—and believe me, I really get it too!"

Ramon adds, "After I did the Ninth Step, that feeling of impending doom finally lifted.

Now when it comes back, I check to make sure if there's more Ninth Step work for me to do. If there isn't, I know it's my insanity and I do a quick Second Step!"

Despite the lure of the promises, Step Nine can seem formidable the first time around. Dealing with people we have hurt can be a frightening prospect. Recovering people who ignore the red flags and rush into this step usually end up wishing they had moved more cautiously.

As you look over your Eighth Step list, consider some of the following questions:

1. Am I sincere about my amends? Sometimes our misdeeds are our hostile response to harm that was done to us. Can we let that go now, or will our anger turn our amends into an opportunity to recall someone else's wrongs?

2. Is this the right time to make amends? Would it be better to make them later on? Considering the current circumstances of the person to whom I am making amends, would it be more sensitive to postpone the amends to a later date?

3. Are my amends realistic? Am I confident that I am working on the character defects that led me to hurt the person to whom I am making amends? If I am making an amends to someone to whom I owe money, am I able to return the money now? Am I

likely to stick to the repayment plan I am offering?

4. What is the most appropriate, most loving way to handle this amends? How comfortable am I dealing face-to-face? Person-to-person visits, though awkward at first, are usually the most effective. But there can be compelling reasons when a phone call or a letter would be more effective.

5. Many times we have evaded making amends because we imagine some potential damage that just isn't there. But there are occasions when an amends might embarrass or even hurt the person to whom we are making the amends. If, for instance, we have felt remorse for flirting (or more than flirting) with a best friend's boyfriend or girlfriend, making an amends is bound to hurt our best friend's feelings and damage the relationships as well!

Sometimes amends may even result in difficult consequences for ourselves. For instance, if we have broken the law, will coming clean put us in a legal situation we are not ready to deal with?

Whatever the circumstances, or the feelings, or the consequences, *always* discuss your amends with a sponsor, a counselor, or another trusted person. The insights and the advice you get can help you avoid the pitfalls that can come with this step.

If we take time to think and talk about each amends, our amends making is bound to be a rewarding experience. More often than not, the person to whom we are making the amends is more than welcoming—and almost always sees our commitment to sobriety as all the amends that are needed.

► **"I felt so powerful after I did this step, like there wasn't anything to be really afraid of ever again."**

Sometimes, however, we encounter a hostile response. Ramon points out his experiences with handling that. "Most of my family accepted my amends and that was great," he says. "But one uncle I'd hurt rejected my amends. He said that no matter how sober I got, I'd always be rotten. It hurt, but I didn't get angry. I knew his holding on to a grudge was about him, not about me. I felt so powerful after I did this step, like there wasn't anything to be really afraid of ever again."

As Janine says, "There were a lot of amends I had to make for things I did that came straight out of the alcohol. Like the time I threw up in someone's car. It was awful. But I'd already cleaned up the mess. I just hadn't said how bad I felt about it and how sorry I was for embarrassing my girlfriend in front of her mother. So when I made the amends I explained it was because I had a drinking problem. Even though *everyone* in my neighborhood knew I had one heck of a drinking problem, no one had heard me admit it. I told them I was in a Twelve Step program and hadn't had a drink in six months. Chelsea's mom said that was amends enough."

▶ **"It's like all the amendments to the Constitution. When you amend it, you change it. When I make amends, it's like changing me."**

"I had to make a financial amends to my mom," Ramon adds. "Since I was ten, I'd taken money from her wallet so I could pay for drugs and booze. She never knew about it, and I wasn't sure how much I'd taken, but it had to be hundreds of dollars, which I didn't have. But I still needed to make the amends. My sponsor helped me make up a plan to pay her back, five bucks a week for a year. Which wasn't all that easy because I was fourteen when I got sober and how do you make any money at that age? When I talked to my mom about it, my mom said forget it. She was glad I was sober and that's all that counted. But I insisted, which surprised me even more than it surprised my mom. That's when I understood the amends was for me more than it was for her. I got a job after school and even liked it. It was proof to me that I could change.

"It's like all the amendments to the Constitution," Ramon says. "When you amend it, you change it. When I make amends, it's like changing me."

"An apology is part of making amends," Liz says. "It's how I start, by saying I'm sorry. But an apology only says you're sorry. Making amends says I'm changing. If I'm not ready to change, then I'm not really doing the Ninth Step."

"My stepfather showed me how *not* to make amends," says Bill. "He kept saying how he'd been brought up to believe homosexuals were bad people and it was all *his* folks' fault that he'd kept on saying cruel things about me being gay. He wasn't taking *any* responsibility and that really bugged me. Then when I got into the program and I was making my first amends to my friend, I found I was trying to get him to see how horrible my childhood had been. I was trying to get him to feel sorry for me for not being nicer to him!"

"I let them know that I know I did something I'm really sorry about," Liz explains. "I tell them I really do care about their feelings and that I'm changing so that I never do it again to them or anyone else. Later on we can get into my childhood and my parents, but that's something else. When I do the Ninth Step, I like to keep it pure-and-simple amends and nothing else."

"A couple years ago I got mugged," Derek says. "I got pretty beaten up too. The worst part was, I felt I deserved it. It took a lot of help to make me understand that I didn't. A lot of people feel guilty when something bad happens to them even when it's not their fault. So my main point when I make amends is that they didn't deserve to be treated badly. You wouldn't believe how well people take it. It's like no one ever said anything like that to them before.

"I made a play for my best friend's girl," Derek continues. "She went out with me a couple times. My friend never found out, but I felt lousy. When I got sober, I started feeling even more crappy about it. I thought the only way to feel better was to tell my friend. But my friend and the girl were engaged, and my sponsor said I was nuts if I thought I'd feel better for telling people something that was going to make them feel worse. The only thing I could do was pray that I would never do anything so dumb like that again. I haven't and it works. I mean, I feel okay about it now."

Janine adds, "I needed to make amends to my boyfriend, and it was in showing him how much I really cared about his feelings and learning how much he cared about mine, that we started thinking about getting married. You just can't have a good relationship unless there's room for amends-making in it!"

Very often we fear that people whom we have harmed will never want to be close with us again even if they do accept our amends. It would be foolish to deny that can happen. It's also true we don't always wish to be friends with people we make our amends to. But it is impressive how often making amends can strengthen a friendship.

As Bill says, "The kinds of friends I make today are people who can accept my being human—and that means my not being perfect. It means being able to say you're sorry, that you make mistakes, that you care, and that you're growing and changing. It took me a lot of work to learn how to accept other people's amends sincerely. It's what makes relationships good."

In affirming other people's worth, in affirming their right to feel good about themselves, we are also affirming our own worth. In dealing squarely with other people, we are learning how to deal squarely with ourselves. Fair, honest, loving relationships are possible now. Our past can be a tool now rather than a weapon. We can free ourselves now from yesterday's regret and remorse—and open ourselves to the abundance of today and tomorrow.

But check out pages 83-84 of the Big Book, *Alcoholics Anonymous*. Make sure *all* the promises are working in your life now. You deserve it!

STEP 10

Continued to take personal inventory and when we were wrong promptly admitted it.

"When I used, I spent half my time doing nothing but thinking about me and the other half telling everyone how sorry I was," Ramon laughs. "I told my sponsor I'd been practicing this step all my life."

Janine goes on: "All the other steps looked a little spooky at first. This one looked more user-friendly, if you know what I mean."

Many of us know just what Janine means. No matter what our drinking and drugging history was like, it's thanks to our *sober* history that we can approach this step without anxiety.

After all, in our Fourth Step we learned that personal inventories were far from fatal. In our Ninth, we discovered we could make amends and not feel as if we were groveling. No matter how anxious we had been at first, we saw how these steps opened new doors to our own happiness, how they had become essential tools to our well-being—and there was nothing fearful about that!

The Tenth Step is often described as one of the "maintenance" steps. All too often, people mistakenly interpret it as an "optional" step: try it if you feel like it someday. It could very well be that because Step Ten holds no terror, we tend to underestimate its power—as well as the very real challenge it holds. As one old-timer said, "Most of the steps look a lot harder than they are. The Tenth Step is a fooler. It's harder than it looks."

Getting sober is a remarkable achievement. An alcoholic or addict who can stay off booze and drugs for ninety days has a lot to be proud of. But the statistics remind us that it's even more remarkable to stay sober for years, even decades. The longtime winners almost invariably point to the Tenth Step as key to their sustained recovery.

What's easy about the Fourth and Fifth, the Eighth and Ninth Steps, is that once they're over, they're over for a while. Few people go back to them more than once a year or so. What's hard about the so-called maintenance steps is the discipline needed to go back to them every day.

We do a Fourth Step or a Ninth Step when something isn't right with us. We do the maintenance steps even when everything's fine. For problem-oriented folks like us, that can be hard to understand—until we realize that the maintenance steps keep us right one day at a time. Practicing them daily keeps us out of the trouble and depression and confusion that used to plague us every drinking, drugging day.

Here's our chance to see who we are on a daily basis. Were we civil to our parents in the morning, or were we our usual impatient selves? Were we late for our job or school? Were we well prepared? Were we doing a bit of self-sabotage by not being prepared? If so, is that getting to be chronic?

The day goes on. Did we pay attention, or were we bored or irritated? Did we feel productive and happy, or did we feel frustrated again and again?

Did we go to a meeting? Was it interesting? Did we get something out of it, or are we starting to feel a little bored there? Should we look around for another meeting? Maybe we should consider other points of our program: Have we talked to our sponsor this week? What are we doing spiritually? Did we pray and meditate? Or do the First Step?

If we socialized, did we have fun? Was it good being with friends and family, or were we shy? Or did we find the kids boring? If someone there was drinking, did that make us uncomfortable—or perhaps just plain bored? We should check on our dealings in our relationships. We should dwell a bit on how that special relationship is going. Are there problems or difficult feelings?

Although we use the Tenth Step to spot problems in the making, more often than not we come away full of gratitude for several things. First, the improvements we are seeing in our lives one day at a time. Second, the peacefulness we feel within us. And third, our evolving faith in a higher power. And just in case we forgot that the joy of living is the theme of being sober, why not check out if we enjoyed ourselves today?

That's just a guideline that you may want to keep in mind as you do your first Tenth Step work. It's hard to imagine the most dedicated recovering people going over their days in such detail. It's just not necessary. What is necessary, however, is that we get into the habit of giving ourselves a serious look. We need to remember that fudging small details can lead to big problems later on.

▶ **"If I don't do my Tenth Step, I can sweep a lot of crap under the carpet. Crap I've got to deal with or I'm not going to stay sober."**

As Bill points out, "Maybe it doesn't matter to other folks what any one day is like. For me, as an alcoholic and drug addict, it's different. I don't wait till things get bad to start drinking and taking drugs. I drink and use while things are on their way toward getting bad. I've got this thing called denial," he adds with a chuckle, "and if I don't do my Tenth Step, I can sweep a lot of crap under the carpet. Crap I've got to deal with or I'm not going to stay sober."

Adds Liz, "When it comes to relapses, I'm just as likely to drink over a broken heart as a broken date—or even a broken nail. From doing my Tenth Step I know what's going on in my life, I share it at meetings, I share it with my sponsors. This way things don't get out of hand, and problems get solved before they become high drama or even tragedy."

There's no rule as to when or how often we are to do the Tenth Step. But it's clear that we have to do it regularly for it to make a real impact on our lives. All we need to do is pick a time—once a day—when we know we'll be free and a place where we know we won't be interrupted. Before bed seems to be the most popular time.

Some people write in a diary. Some scribble a note or two. But it's perfectly okay to go over the preceding twenty-four hours while on the way to school or work . . . or lying in bed with our hands folded underneath our heads. Experiment a little and you'll come up with what's most comfortable for you.

"At first I thought, 'Wow, another chance to look into those defects,'" Liz says. "But most of the time it's more like a chance to pat myself on the back. Before the Tenth Step I thought nothing much was happening in my life. Now, every day, I can really see the progress I'm making."

The Tenth Step is also an opportunity to spot recurring problems—and to look for possible character defects behind them. Are we having trouble with anger? With money? With procrastination? Are we seeing certain patterns of behavior we don't like? Yes, it hurts to look at these things. But it'll hurt a lot worse if we don't.

"I was always having trouble in school," Derek says. "It got better when I got sober, but it still wasn't good. I tried to pretend it was no big deal. When I got to the Tenth Step, I got real about how discouraging it was for me, doing so badly in school. Being a bad student was a big part of my feeling like a bad person. The guidance counselor had me do some testing, and it turns out I've got a serious reading dysfunction. It's just more realistic for me to do my best at school, and to understand how to build on my strengths. After graduation, I'm going to trade school and I'm going to get work that I'll really like! I feel real good about myself. That's the promises working in my own life."

As for the amends part, that's almost easy now. We all know, from our own experience, that the longer a problem goes unattended, the worse it gets. But when we drank and drugged, we tended to spend hours and hours rationalizing and justifying our behavior instead of making amends quickly and moving on with our lives.

Now when we do our daily inventory, we can spot our errors. If we make our apology for it right away, we can usually keep a situation from developing. Almost always there just aren't any terrible consequences if we acknowledge right away that we have been in the wrong—and own up to it.

More often than not, it's no more than a casual, "I'm sorry that I raised my voice just now," followed by some assurance that it wasn't *the other person's* fault.

▶ **"Doing the Tenth Step was a real change for me, because it meant I had to take today more seriously than yesterday."**

"I borrowed some money from a guy at work," Bill explains, "and I couldn't pay it back when I said I would. Instead of waiting till the guy got steamed and came to me, I went to him right away and explained the situation. He said it was no problem waiting another week. But I know that if I hadn't apologized for being late, the situation could have become real trouble."

When our error is a response, or maybe even a defense, to what we perceive to be someone else's wrong, we have to be willing to dig a little deeper into who we are—and what our underlying defect may be. Otherwise, our so-called apology may sound more like, "I'm sorry you nag so much," or "I'm sorry you don't have an honest bone in your body."

In those cases we have to make some decisions. Since they're decisions we'll live with, let's be sure to give them the thought they deserve. For instance, if we have snapped angrily at someone for correcting something we did, we have to come to terms with how overly sensitive we are to criticism.

If we are overly critical of our friends, we might have to examine why we don't make friends with people we esteem. At one time we could dwell interminably on the defects of our friends. Now we have to look inside ourselves and ask what we are doing with people we don't like.

Are we beginning to see some patterns here? Is there something here for our next Fourth Step? Is there a defect here that we can take directly to the Sixth and Seventh Steps?

For many recovering alcoholics and drug addicts, the Tenth Step turns the slogan One Day at a Time into a philosophy for living. Janine says, "When I got sober, I thought 'one day at a time' was pathetic. I couldn't imagine me falling so low that I could only make it 'one day at a time.' I had big plans about working at the bank, promotion by promotion. I was proud that I was living twenty years at a time. Which in addition to not making meetings explains why I slipped after ninety days. When I came back I started to not drink one day at a time. Then I started to do school one day at a time. And then I did my relationship one day at a time too instead of when we're married and have kids and we live in the suburbs. So I'm living one day at a time instead of in the future. I've got a great future but I don't live in it anymore. The Tenth Step is the way I remember what day it is and that I'm supposed to be in it!"

"I was just the opposite," Bill says. "I was always living in the past. Everything was all about how my dad deserted us when I was little and how I got this terrible stepfather. It might look like I was living in the present, but really my head was a hundred years ago. Doing the Tenth Step was a real change for me, because it meant I had to take today more seriously than yesterday."

The Tenth Step is also a reminder of how the tools help us make the changes we need to make in order to get sober and stay that way. As Ramon says, "What's the point in being sober if you're going to be miserable? For me learning to stay sober was a lot about learning to be happy. The Tenth Step makes sure I don't forget how important my happiness and my comfort are one day at a time."

STEP 11

> *Sought through prayer and meditation to improve our conscious contact with God* as we understood God, *praying only for knowledge of God's will* for us and the power to carry that out.*

If you've been to more than a handful of Twelve Step meetings, you've already heard that the steps are in their order for a reason. When it comes to Step Eleven, it's clear why that one comes toward the end. If it came any earlier, we probably wouldn't be able to believe it.

As Jerry says, "Prayer and meditation is for people a lot older than I am. Whoever heard of a fifteen-year-old meditating, anyway?"

---

*The change here to ". . . God *as we understood God,* praying only for knowledge of God's will . . ." is an adaptation of the original Eleventh Step of the Twelve Steps of Alcoholics Anonymous. The original reads " . . . God *as we understood Him,* praying only for knowledge of His will . . ." The original Twelve Steps of Alcoholics Anonymous are reprinted in their entirety at the back of this book.

As Traci says, "Well, I've always believed in prayer, even when I was using. But meditation is something for *other* religions. I just don't think of Presbyterians meditating!"

Derek says, "I thought meditation was like Zen or Buddhism. It just doesn't sound very *American,* if you know what I mean."

Finally, Ellie says, "I meditated a lot when I was stoned. I just never imagined it was something I'd do *after* I got clean!"

As incredible as it might seem, everyone can meditate—including sober American teenagers.

▶ **"I meditated a lot when I was stoned. I just never imagined it was something I'd do <u>after</u> I got clean!"**

As we found with the Third Step, it's a matter of belief and experience. If someone tells a small child that he'll burn himself if he touches a stove, he'll *know* it's so—because someone told him. But he won't *believe* it until he touches it himself and gets hurt. If someone tells us that drinking is bad (and someone is bound to have said that to each of us), we'll know it's true. But we really don't believe it until we end up in trouble ourselves.

So it seems that believing is a combination of knowing plus our own experience. For instance, we've probably heard a million times that sobriety would be good for us, but how many of us believed it until after we had already had some experience with it?

It's the same with prayer and meditation. If we've had no experience with either one of them, it's understandable that many of us would push them away, almost out of hand—no matter how enthusiastic other people seem to be about them. Then one day we realized there was something those other people had that we were missing out on. Could it be something material, like a job? Or better relationships? Or just a look, not necessarily a glow, that tells us that there's something going on inside them that isn't going on inside us?

Liz tells how she got into the Eleventh Step. "I just didn't see me doing it—or needing it. But I saw this girl at meetings who was *always* looking pretty down and one day she was starting to look a lot more up. So I asked if she had a new boyfriend, and she just laughed and said she was doing the Eleventh Step. Well, let's just say it got me thinking."

Derek explains, "I'd gone through the steps, but I still didn't see God as something who really knew who I was or spoke to me directly. I still had this higher power who took care of all drunks, if you know what I mean, but he didn't know me personally. I think I was just feeling incredibly bad about how I was doing at school, and I knew all the friends in the world weren't going to make me feel otherwise. What I needed was my very own, personal, you-know-me-well higher power. So I started praying for one. It wasn't until I started to meditate that I got one."

Prayer, we are told, is talking to God and asking for help. Considering how practiced human beings are in asking, it's surprising that we have so much to learn about how to ask.

"I used to ask for the things that I thought would make me happy," says Bill. "Like a car, and a relationship, and a few extra million too. It wasn't too long before I was seeing a guy I'd met at a gay AA roundup and I had a car too. I couldn't understand why I wasn't happy all the time. I didn't have the millions, it's true, but I figured out by then that they wouldn't make me happy either. So I heard a man saying at a meeting that his higher power had better things planned for him than he could ever imagine, and I decided to try it. So when I prayed, I just asked my higher power to bring me peace. I figured I'd let *him* be the judge of what was the best way for me to have it! I began to see that my happiness wasn't going to come from external things so much but from internal things."

"I was frightened that maybe God didn't really like me so maybe I'd be better off *not* knowing what Her will was for me," says Janine. "But it must have been in my fourth year of sobriety that I got the message that

God wanted only love for me. That's when I started to do the Eleventh Step, when I knew Her will for me just *had* to be good news."

Ramon laughs as he identifies with Janine. "I guess I figured there were some people God wanted to be rich and famous and happy," he says, "which meant *some people* had to be poor and unfamous and miserable. Considering my luck before I got to the program, I figured I knew which end I was supposed to be at. Then my sponsor challenged me about that. He said I should check it out with God first. Which is how I started to make conscious contact with a higher power. It's how I found out that my higher power thinks there's plenty for *everyone* if we'd only believe it."

▶ **"I was frightened that maybe God didn't really like me so maybe I'd be better off <u>not</u> knowing what Her will was for me."**

Prayer and meditation, like all the other tools of recovery, are intensely *practical*. Like all tools, they work better the more we use them. That takes time and it takes practice. From the very beginning, however, people get results. It's just that the results keep getting better as we move along.

How we pray and how we meditate are very personal matters. Everyone has a particular way. But as we move into Step Eleven for the first time, it can be helpful to ask other people how they go about it. Keep in mind that there's no right way or wrong way here, and that no one way is better than any other. Many people, in fact, consider prayer just a way of talking to their higher power—even if they're still not very comfortable with the higher power concept.

"I tell my higher power how I'm feeling that day," says Janine. "I tell HP first how my body is feeling. Then I talk about what my feelings are like. I try to get very real about what I'm anxious about and it doesn't matter how small it seems. Then I ask HP to lift all the barriers that keep me from feeling really good, and then I ask HP to help me and everyone else. Sometimes, just before I meditate, I ask HP to let me see myself and others through Her eyes rather than my own. That helps a lot too."

"I still ask for what I want," says Derek. "Like I want all my legal problems *behind* me forever. I figure my higher power knows me better than I do so there's no point in pretending I don't want things when I do. But I always end my prayers with 'Thy will, not mine, be done.' So that if I don't get something, I'll understand why it's better for me not to have whatever it is, at least right then. To me being spiritual means being open-minded and looking for the gifts in things, even though there are days when I have to look very, very hard."

101

Bill adds, "I always end by asking God to take care of everyone. I used to say 'especially the people I love.' Then I heard it helped if you prayed for people you were mad at or afraid of, so I'd say 'especially the people I love and the people I hate.' But that sounded funny so now I just tell God their names and say I want them to feel peace in their lives."

▶ **The most important, and also the most challenging, aspect of meditation is clearing your head of all distracting thoughts and plans and feelings. That way the mind will be all the more receptive to what your higher power has to say.**

Whereas prayer is *talking* to higher power, meditation is often described as *listening* to higher power. For almost everyone, that comes less easily—but for those who try it on a consistent basis, the rewards are extraordinary.

The most important, and also the most challenging, aspect of meditation is clearing your head of all distracting thoughts and plans and feelings. That way the mind will be all the more receptive to what your higher power has to say.

First, make sure your space is free of distraction. Find a place where no one will interrupt you. Close the door. Take the phone off the hook. Close the window if there's traffic outside. If you decide to play music, make sure it's music that you won't get caught up in. Check out the meditation section of your local CD store. You can find anything from classical music to recordings of waves crashing along the shore to help get you in the right frame of mind.

Sit down—in a chair, on the floor, whichever is more comfortable. Cross your knees if that makes you more comfortable. Lie down, if you're sure you won't go to sleep.

Close your eyes and start to clear your mind. Concentrate on the music or concentrate on your breathing. Try to keep your mind from getting all wrapped up in what you're planning to do after supper or the math test yesterday or how angry you are at your mother and father.

Just be. And breathe. And listen to the tape if you are playing one.

Doing that for a whole minute can be taxing the first time out. But as we give it a try, day after day, it becomes easier and our meditation sessions become longer and more peaceful.

Will you hear your higher power speak in words? Some people have, but more often, there's no "message." At first that may be disappointing to those who had hoped for a complete item-by-item blueprint of God's plan for them. As we move along in our sobriety, however, we will know that the thoughts and ideas that come to us when we are feeling peaceful are the ones to trust, the ones our higher power wants us to heed. It's the ones that come to us when we are fearful and angry that we must resist!

"Like my worrying about getting into college," Liz says. "It got so bad I was up every night making myself sick about it. One night I decided to do the Eleventh Step. At one point I just got this feeling that I just wasn't supposed to suffer anymore. From then on, I just felt a lot better about accepting whatever life held in store for me."

Ramon adds, "Doing the Eleventh Step helps me remember that I'm not in charge of the world. If something's not going the way I think it should, I don't beat up on myself. I just do the Eleventh Step, and I find that maybe things are supposed to work out *another* way instead."

"I worry a lot about other people," says Ellie, "especially my family, because everyone else in my family is drinking. I feel so helpless and so guilty that even though I'm not smoking pot, there's not anything I can do for them. When I do the Eleventh Step, I find out what I forgot since the last time I did it, that staying sober is the best thing I can do for myself *and* for them too."

Over and over again, recovering people agree that being sober is what their higher power wants most for them. It's how the good things started to happen—and it's where the good things still come from.

STEP 12

Having had a spiritual awakening as the result of these steps, we tried to carry this message to alcoholics, and to practice these principles in all our affairs.

It's the step that embodies all the other steps, the step that culminates inevitably in the joy of living. It's the step that you see far, far out on the horizon, almost beyond your reach. It's also the one step you may have experienced *before* you came into recovery. Not as a doer, as a recipient.

Twelve-Stepping: It means confronting an active alcoholic or drug abuser with the problem, explaining you've been there too, showing that there is a way out. It's sharing your experience, strength, and hope, carrying the message of recovery, offering a way out of suffering.

If you were Twelve-Stepped, you might remember it as embarrassing, perhaps even shameful and infuriating. But you may also remember that the people who came to you had something you wanted. Even though it was hard to believe you would ever have it too, you wanted it enough to take a chance.

While the Twelfth Step is usually seen as a call to action, it's also an affirmation of your growing consciousness of spirituality in your life. As you look over the months you've been sober, you're bound to see spirituality in your life from the very first day of your recovery.

The way to prove to yourself that you have it is to give it away. If you weren't able to give it away, you wouldn't be sure you had it. As you're bound to hear, giving it away is the only way to keep it too! It all seems paradoxical, but remember that the Twelve Steps are first and foremost *practical*. The Twelfth Step is like all the other steps: if it didn't work, no one would bother with it.

▶ **While the Twelfth Step is usually seen as a call to action, it's also an affirmation of your growing consciousness of spirituality in your life.**

How we go about our Twelfth Step work will determine our success with it. If we go about "converting" people to "our way of life," the spirit of "You'll be better when you're like me" is bound to come through—and hurt the people we are trying to help. All we can do is share who we are, where we've come from, and how it is for us now. If people ask for our help, we can provide it happily. But if people are wary of us, our "message" will be more like an affliction than a gift.

As ardently as we believe that to be true for us, we can't help feeling uncomfortable telling others it's what they should be doing with their lives. No one knows better than alcoholics the pain and put-down of an unwelcome "What you need is" or a "You should do that." Besides, doesn't one of AA's traditions state that AA works by attraction rather than promotion?

Not surprisingly, the solution to our confusion and discomfort lies in the step itself. The "message" that the Twelfth Step refers to is clearly *not* "You should get sober" but rather "Having had a spiritual awakening as a result of these steps . . ." So when we see others suffering from our disease, we're not asked to tell them to sober up or to tell them that they'll be better off when they're more like us.

The message turns out to be that they are loveable and deserving. We can invite them to see themselves, as we try to see ourselves, through the loving eyes of our higher power rather than through our own (sometimes) righteous, even antagonistic eyes. We are called on to make a connection by sharing our stories, telling how bad it was for us, how hopeless we felt, and how that changed. If they are interested in pursuing a sober path, we can help, but we can't turn them into sober people. We can carry the message; we can't carry the drunk.

Sometimes we will meet someone who is ready, even eager, to hear our message. Many times we do not. But if we have acted in the spirit of our higher power, we will always be better for our Twelfth Step work, no matter what its apparent effect on others has been.

Too many young people throughout the world are already suffering from alcoholism and drug addiction. Nowadays we know that no one is too young to recover from alcoholism. We know too that no one has to hit the terrible bottoms that were once considered almost essential before beginning recovery.

▶ **"It's an awakening. I wouldn't have called it spiritual, but why not, if it helps me so much."**

No one can carry the message more effectively to today's drug-addicted and alcoholic teenagers than other young people who are in recovery. You can make yourself available to young newcomers you see at meetings. You can visit detox units and rehabs. You can even visit prisons. But the perils can be as great as the need. More than one recovering person has gone, unprepared, on a Twelfth Step call and wound up drinking.

Before setting out on Twelfth Step work, make sure you're ready. Talk it over with your sponsor. See if you're feeling really comfortable with it—or if you're just trying to do the "right" thing. Remember that the really "right" thing is that your own sense of well-being and sobriety come first.

Go with someone else from the program. No matter how old and experienced, no one should do Twelfth Step calls alone.

Be real. No one has a better nose for a phony than a drunk. If you announce that you've been blissed out since the moment you put down the drink and the drug, your listener may think you're still on something!

Don't overcommit yourself. For all its rewards, Twelfth Step work *is* work.

Most important, remember that Twelfth Step work isn't all about Twelve-Stepping. Being active in a group, making coffee, chairing a meeting—all count as Twelfth Step work. So does giving a special welcome to a newcomer, listening to someone share about problems, and sharing your own experience, strength, and hope.

Some of the most successful Twelfth Step work we do is work we are totally unaware we did. As Derek says, "When I got out of rehab and started going to meetings, I held back from my old crowd. Some of them were still drinking and that wasn't good for me. Frankly, most of them didn't seem too interested in me either. Then one day, this kid, one of the drinkers, asks me if he could talk to me after school. It turned out he was coming to me for help about getting sober. Then he said it was just from seeing me doing so well that got him interested. And all the time I was being Mr. Low Profile too!"

"Every time I do something that I wouldn't have done when I was drinking is Twelfth Step work as far as I'm concerned," Ramon says. "Like I used to steal money from my mom every chance I got. Now I have a job three days a week after school, bagging groceries over at the market. I have a higher power today who says I don't have to steal or lie in order to be okay. That's practicing these principles, isn't it?"

"Like when someone came into the garage, I used to say things, really rotten things, under my breath about them," Bill admits. "I used to think it was just funny, you know. I thought it kind of helped me let off some steam. But it isn't funny and there's better ways of letting off steam. Now that I like myself better, I don't notice other people's defects so much. I'm just seeing lots of things about me that I never imagined were there. It's an awakening. I wouldn't have called it spiritual, but why not, if it helps me so much."

For most recovering people, young and old and in between, practicing these principles in all our affairs means turning to all the steps more and more. Now that the old tricks—getting stoned, getting wasted, getting mad, getting even—don't work for us, we're often at a loss of what to do instead. If it weren't for the guidance the program offers, many would have almost no other option *except* to return to alcohol and other drugs.

"Doing the Twelfth Step means doing all the other steps," Ramon says. "The longer I'm sober, the more experience I have with the steps, the more I trust them too. Every day there must be three or four times when I say to myself, 'Third Step' or 'Eleventh Step.' It's not like I'm *against* using other tools. It's just that they don't work for me the way these tools do.

▶ **"Today I don't just know I've got a disease, I really accept it. I know if I go back out there things are going to get bad <u>right</u> away."**

"The things I've learned, I wouldn't have ever learned at home," he goes on. "It's not like they're holding back or anything. They just don't know it. After all, they grew up in dysfunctional homes too. When my mom has a problem and I suggest something like turning it over or keeping the focus on herself, it's like news to her!"

"I still have problems," Janine says. "I still worry too much too. But I don't have any worries I can't handle, and I don't have a problem that hasn't been solvable *without a drink or a drug*. It's because I'm coming to believe that the steps never let me down. It seemed like I was always getting a bum lead *all the time.* Now I have something I trust and I never had that before."

"The only hitch is you got to do sobriety *every* day," Ramon laughs. "Even if I don't get to a meeting, I'm *always* doing the first three steps every single morning."

"Or calling a friend," Janine adds.

"Or my sponsor," says Jerry.

"If I don't do something, I'm putting myself in a real bad spot," says Janine, not laughing anymore. "Today I don't just know I've got a disease, I really accept it. I know if I go back out there things are going to get bad *right* away. You go back to where you left off. That's what the people coming back from a slip say, and I know that from experience. I wanted to die at the end of my drinking. If I go out there, I might be in a car wreck. I could wind up in the wrong neighborhood, very late at night, and it could be awful. I could be raped. I could get myself killed."

"I wouldn't have to wait for an accident," Ramon says. "I could kill myself, like my brother did. AA didn't just show me *how* to live. It's given me a reason *why* to live and my brother didn't have that."

The dire consequences exist for all active alcoholics and drug addicts, no matter what age. But thanks to the meetings, the people, and the steps, alcoholics and other drug addicts can lead productive, contented lives.

"Like they say," Ellie says, "it works if you work it."

As Ramon adds, "It *is* work, but it's nice work if you can get it."

THE TWELVE STEPS
OF ALCOHOLICS ANONYMOUS*

1. We admitted we were powerless over alcohol—that our lives had become unmanageable.
2. Came to believe that a Power greater than ourselves could restore us to sanity.
3. Made a decision to turn our will and our lives over to the care of God *as we understood Him.*
4. Made a searching and fearless moral inventory of ourselves.
5. Admitted to God, to ourselves, and to another human being the exact nature of our wrongs.
6. Were entirely ready to have God remove all these defects of character.
7. Humbly asked Him to remove our shortcomings.
8. Made a list of all persons we had harmed, and became willing to make amends to them all.
9. Made direct amends to such people wherever possible, except when to do so would injure them or others.
10. Continued to take personal inventory and when we were wrong promptly admitted it.
11. Sought through prayer and meditation to improve our conscious contact with God *as we understood Him,* praying only for knowledge of His will for us and the power to carry that out.
12. Having had a spiritual awakening as the result of these steps, we tried to carry this message to alcoholics, and to practice these principles in all our affairs.

---

*The Twelve Steps of Alcoholics Anonymous are taken from *Alcoholics Anonymous,* 3d ed., published by AA World Services, Inc., New York, N.Y., 59-60. The Twelve Steps of AA are reprinted with permission of Alcoholics Anonymous World Services, Inc. Permission to reprint the Twelve Steps does not mean that AA has reviewed or approved the contents of this publication, nor that AA agrees with the views expressed herein. AA is a program for the recovery from alcoholism. Use of the Twelve Steps in connection with programs and activities that are patterned after AA, but that address other problems, does not imply otherwise.

THE PROMISES
OF ALCOHOLICS ANONYMOUS[*]

If we are painstaking about this phase of our development, we will be amazed before we are half way through. We are going to know a new freedom and a new happiness. We will not regret the past nor wish to shut the door on it. We will comprehend the word serenity and we will know peace. No matter how far down the scale we have gone, we will see how our experience can benefit others. That feeling of uselessness and self-pity will disappear. We will lose interest in selfish things and gain interest in our fellows. Self-seeking will slip away. Our whole attitude and outlook upon life will change. Fear of people and of economic insecurity will leave us. We will intuitively know how to handle situations which used to baffle us. We will suddenly realize that God is doing for us what we could not do for ourselves.

---

[*]The Promises of Alcoholics Anonymous are taken from *Alcoholics Anonymous,* 3d ed., published by AA World Services, Inc., New York, N.Y., 83-84. Reprinted with permission of AA World Services, Inc.